cooking at

THE MERCHANT HOUSE

SHAUN HILL

cooking at

THE MERCHANT HOUSE

photography Jason Lowe

conran
OCTOPUS

First published in 2000 by Conran Octopus Limited, a part of Octopus Publishing Group, 2–4 Heron Quays, London E14 4JP www.conran-octopus.co.uk
This paperback edition published in 2004

Editorial Cookery Consultant: Jenni Muir **Art Editor**: Vanessa Courtier **Design Assistant:** Gina Hochstein **Production Controller:** Alex Wiltshire

The publishers would like to thank Claire Clifton, Linda Collister and Marion Moisy for their assistance in producing this title, as well as Stuart Cooper, Lynn Bryan and Claire Wrathall.

British Library Cataloguing-in-Publication Data. A catalogue record for this book is available from the British Library ISBN 1 84091 398 3

Colour origination by Sang Choy International, Singapore. Printed and bound in China.

IMPORTANT NOTES FOR READERS

The names and types of ingredients expressed in brackets are for the benefit of American and Australasian readers who have a different cookery language from Britain and are not always able to buy the same products. Australasian readers please note that this book features 8floz imperial cup measurements and 15ml tablespoon (equal to 3 teaspoons). The pint measures are British and equivalent to 20floz; Americans should use the cup measurements given instead. British readers are usually required to use medium-size eggs in these recipes, which are of equivalent size to the large eggs of the USA, hence the word large being given here in brackets after the word medium. Readers can use any type of measurement they feel comfortable with, however it is important not to switch between units of measurement while cooking as the quantities given are not exact conversions, nor should they be. The purpose of conversions is to allow people to easily use their preferred units of measurement, not to present them with an exact translation of grams to ounces and cups.

Contents

Introduction

Every successful dinner party host has thought of turning professional. The guests all think your tarte fine aux pommes is a knockout and everyone is certain their friends would flock to your restaurant. With £40 or more a head the going rate for even the average provincial restaurant, there must be a fortune waiting for anyone with talent...

The beauty is that there is an element of truth in this fantasy. You need no professional certificates to set up a restaurant and indeed there are a number of dreary, mediocre eateries plying their trade with apparent success. Providing someone turns up at your restaurant to eat and pay, what appears on the plate will define your success and how much it costs to put there will decide how long you remain in business.

The pitfalls are mainly financial. The food in a restaurant is charged for and this colours the relationship with those dining. Unlike guests in your home, customers will whinge and bellyache if they don't like the grub. You also need to make a profit. The heating, crockery, cutlery and table linen you take for granted at home must be costed into the equation and gradual replacements taken into account. The amount you spend setting up shop has to be repaid to the bank, too, and can amount to significant sums per person served.

All is not lost, however. Those like myself who do this for a living are regularly the least appropriate people to be in charge of a business. Professional chefs by the nature of things cook when they are not hungry. They see the food as a vehicle for craftmanship and can spend hours teasing and torturing some innocent piece of fish in order that a bizarre aesthetic may be fulfilled. Many will have specialized in a particular skill like fish cookery or sauces but have little knowledge of pastry work or vegetable preparation. Very few are good at every aspect of the job and, even if they were, it is personal taste as much as technical expertise that will be the deciding factor. The discerning diner is at an advantage in at least knowing what the final product should be like. My own

business acumen is virtually non-existent, by the way, and it should be some consolation to anyone starting down the same path that, despite this, The Merchant House remains in the black.

In 1994 I was working as head chef at Gidleigh Park hotel but recognized it was time for a change. I was getting stale and needed to make a move before my feet gave up. There are only two possible futures for people who chef for a living. One is to become an administrator, someone who delegates and uses their experience to run things well. The other is to get smaller and cook more. There was only one possible choice for me and my wife Anja. We have no wish to be millionaires, but do want to make our own decisions. If I had stayed at Gidleigh Park another five or six years I would have felt too cosy to move, stuck in a well-travelled rut. I needed to get out while I could still do the jobs of two people.

The convention is that the best place to open a restaurant is right next to another one. It demonstrates some local demand you see. Or, if in some beauty spot, then a hotel makes a good base so that the customers may be imported from the Home Counties or sophisticated cities abroad. Our move to Ludlow provoked some serious head-shaking from the great and the good of the restaurant trade. The underlying notion was that provincial

dwellers do not rate money spent on restaurant food as a sound investment whereas the effete and trendy urban type just might. Ludlow had little in the way of restaurants at the time. The principal eaterie was, as for generations past, the Feathers Hotel, a wonderful building like a baroque Christmas cake, but with dire food and the air of a redundant council office by way of atmosphere.

In fact, the Welsh Marches – the border country of which Ludlow is capital – is one of Britain's last undiscovered treats. In the Middle Ages, Ludlow was at the centre of wealth, power and political intrigue, the administrative capital for Wales and flush with profits from the wool and cloth trades. Richard III liked it so much that he kept his nephews in the town's castle before their transfer to the Tower of London, and records show that the Black Prince was able to borrow £120 from a local merchant – which could buy a great deal more than a meal for three back then. Much of the town is authentically medieval, black and white, or elegant Georgian in architecture, but now Ludlow is becoming an attraction for reasons gastronomic as there are more restaurants sporting a food guide gong here than anywhere else outside the capital.

Fascinating though all this history and town planning may be, it was marginal in my own choice of Ludlow to set up the restaurant. I had visited the town and the area around it years ago because it was the setting for so many of AE Housman's *Shropshire Lad* poems. It was sympathetic to a chef's needs, with a thriving market of good food and people who come to buy it. Good things grow round here. There are game and fish to be had and first-rate lines of supply for those times of the year when there is little locally. Just as important, there is an interest in food as an ingredient rather than just produce. People like to eat well and will even pay modest sums to that end. God bless them. That's my kind of town.

Breadmaking

The first indication of what is on offer at mealtime is the bread basket. People are hungriest when they arrive and tastebuds are at their peak, so it is important to get your best shots in early. Cold bread may be easier to digest, but it tastes boring. Lightly textured breads and rolls, freshly warmed, suit large meals better, especially when three or four courses need to be negotiated.

People often shy away from breadmaking because they perceive it to be messy or time-consuming. It's not, nor is it a question of hard work, you just need to plan to make it in advance of eating or, better still, establish a routine.

Learning how to make bread is in any case central to becoming a good cook. The habit of looking and touching rather than slavishly following recipes builds confidence and an understanding of ingredients and cooking processes. Unless you are working in laboratory conditions with absolute control of room temperature, draught exclusion and suchlike, you will be forced to assess each stage of the breadmaking process personally and individually. The dough which rises quite rapidly on a warm summer day may take hours on a chill winter evening. Yet there is no mystery to breadmaking. Old and stale yeast, or even old and stale flour, will spoil the bread. Excessive heat kills the yeast. Avoid both pitfalls and the rest can be mastered.

Bread is largely flour and water, although it is usually tasteless without salt. The ingredient that converts this mixture from pancake to cottage loaf is the raising agent, and the preparation method will be dictated by whether it is yeast, sourdough or baking soda that is used. As elsewhere in cooking, it is difficult to make good food from inferior ingredients. If bread is mostly flour, then a bland, mass-market variety will not produce rolls any better than those bought in a shop. After all, part of the reason for making bread yourself is to achieve something better, not just something fresher or cheaper.

It is difficult to make good food from inferior ingredients.

At The Merchant House we offer two types of bread with a meal, usually fantail rolls (page 14) and a brown flour baguette (page 17). In theory, you could happily give a choice of around four by adding a soda bread and a sourdough. Generally, however, I am not a fan of huge bread baskets filled with cold bread. Usually what the restaurants are offering in these cases is ten variations of white dough, each spruced up with a different flavour – olive and tomato perhaps, or sesame seeds and dried fruit. In essence, these are closely related in flavour and texture. I'd rather devote attention to having the bread at its most appetising rather than give a misleading impression of generous choice.

Kneading and proving bread dough

When the flour, yeast and liquid have been mixed into a dough, it must be kneaded until smooth. The idea is to stretch the gluten in the flour so the gas that the yeast produces can be trapped, lifting the dough.

Flour varies from brand to brand and some absorb more liquid than others. Start off with a soft, slack mixture, reserving a little of the recipe's flour. You can add more flour as you go to no ill effect but adding more water is difficult.

The method for kneading is this: flatten the dough by pushing it forward with the palm and heel of your hand, then fold it back toward you with your fingers. This should be done full force, leaning and pushing against the dough with all your strength.

How long it takes for the dough to rise or prove will depend on the warmth of the place you leave it. Nothing terrible will happen if you leave it in the fridge overnight to prove, otherwise an airing cupboard will do the trick in an hour. In an average kitchen, at summer temperatures, it will take about two hours. You can vary the time to suit yourself. Many experienced breadmakers prefer to let the dough prove slowly as it gives a more developed flavour to the finished loaf. Don't leave the rising dough uncovered for it will dry out. Plastic wrap is ideal, alternatively brush a little oil over the surface.

Knocking back is not, as it sounds, a jolly drinking expression, but sadly only a means of letting gas escape from risen dough. You manage this by punching the bloated dough and kneading it once or twice. The idea is that the dough should then be shaped, left to rise once more, and finally baked.

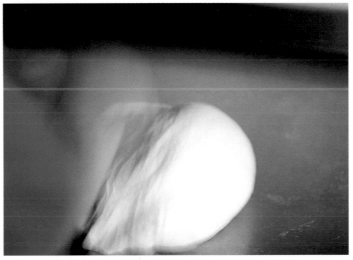

FANTAIL ROLLS

These are our standard white rolls for the restaurant. They are crisp and yet soft and break into segments good for scooping up sauces. They were originally called New England buttermilk rolls and came from a cookbook I bought 20 years ago, never having made bread before and desperate to find something not too difficult. But the recipe has moved and mutated over the years.

First buttermilk became awkward to find, so we used a mixture of skimmed milk and cream of tartar instead, then we eliminated the teaspoon of bicarbonate of soda called for in the original recipe because it didn't seem necessary. Now my wife Anja, who makes all the bread for The Merchant House, doesn't put cream of tartar in the dough either. The fantail rolls are still my favourite and this recipe has certainly been well practised, if nothing else.

MAKES 15-20 ROLLS

25g (1oz) fresh yeast
  (1 x 1oz cake)
1 teaspoon honey
450ml (16floz/2 cups)
  skimmed milk
750g (1lb 10½oz) strong
  white flour
  (5 cups unbleached
  all-purpose flour)
1 teaspoon salt
75g (3oz/¾ stick) butter
1 medium egg, beaten
  (1 large egg.)

In a bowl, dissolve the yeast and honey in a little of the skimmed milk and leave for 10 minutes to froth.

Pour this liquid, plus the remaining milk, onto the flour and salt and mix to a dough. Knead it for 5 minutes – less if you are using a dough-hook on a mechanical mixer.

Cover with plastic wrap and leave in a warm, draught-free spot for about 1 hour to rise. Meanwhile, melt the butter in a small saucepan and set aside until needed.

Knock back the dough, kneading for a few seconds so that it collapses back to its original volume.

Divide the dough into two pieces and roll out until about 3mm (⅛in) thick. Brush the top of both pieces with the melted butter.

Cut the dough into strips 5cm (2in) wide and lay these strips on top of each other in piles about four strips high. Cut them into squares of 5cm (2in).

Pinch one corner of each square together to seal the layers. Stand the squares, sealed edge downwards, in buttered Yorkshire pudding tins or muffin pans and leave the bread to rise for about 1 hour.

Heat the oven to 220°C (425°F/Gas 7). Dab a little beaten egg across the top of each roll and bake for about 15 minutes, by which time they should be golden brown.

POINTS TO WATCH
The milk in this recipe should be at a temperature between cool and lukewarm rather than just out of the refrigerator. Colder milk will take longer to froth but hotter milk may kill the yeast, so you should err on the side of caution.

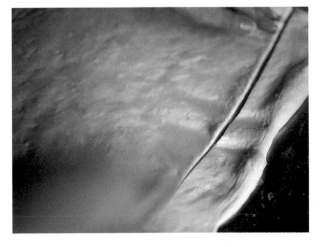

BASIC WHITE ROLLS

If you are a novice, you will find these rolls are good practice for handling the basic ingredients of bread and, of course, will give fine results provided you have bought decent flour. There are plenty of ways to vary this dough too, and we use it to make pizza canapés (page 176).

(page 176)

MAKES 10

50g (2oz / 1/2 stick) butter
175ml (6floz/3/4 cup) milk
25g (1oz) fresh yeast
   (1 x 1oz cake)
1 teaspoon sugar
1 level teaspoon salt
600g (1lb 5oz) strong white
   flour (4 cups unbleached
   all-purpose flour)

Melt the butter. Add the milk and 125ml (4floz/1/2 cup) of water, then heat until the mixture is just lukewarm. Mix in the yeast, then the sugar and salt.

Add almost all the flour (leave a spoonful for dusting the dough as you knead it) and work the mixture into a ball. Cover the dough with plastic wrap and leave until it doubles in bulk, which will probably take a couple of hours.

Knock back the dough by kneading it a few times, then divide into 10 equal pieces. Shape them into balls or cigars and place on a lightly oiled baking tray to prove – this will take only half an hour in a warm kitchen.

Heat the oven to 220°C (425°F/Gas 7) and bake the rolls for 15 minutes. Test for doneness by tapping the base of one of the rolls – it should sound and feel hollow. It will be soggy if underdone and dry if overdone. Leave to cool on a wire rack.

VARIATIONS

Herbs or grated cheese can be added to the dough. Seeds such as poppy or sesame can be sprinkled on top of the rolls just before they are baked, or rye flour can be sifted onto them at the same stage.

This dough makes fine pizza. Roll it out into a couple of large circles and top with Italianate ingredients. Try to leave the rims slightly thicker than the centres so that the topping stays in place. Leave to prove, then bake.

Dried yeast (granules) can be substituted for fresh yeast in this recipe. It has twice the strength of fresh yeast. The packet should give proper instructions, but be sure the granules are not stale otherwise the results will be disappointing.

POINTS TO WATCH

It is crucial that you do not overheat the mixture of butter, milk and water – it must be lukewarm, no higher, in temperature. Let it cool a little before adding the yeast if you are unsure.

Recipes that call for yeast describe the optimum temperature for fermentation as 'blood heat'. Rather than cutting a finger to remind yourself of what this might be, you could place a thermometer into the mixture of yeast, sugar and liquid: 37°C is fine. Alternatively, if you work on the cool side of lukewarm, all will be well.

If the dough doesn't rise you are in trouble. Common culprits are stale yeast or too much heat.

A dough that is too wet will give a heavy, flat result, however it will still be edible.

If the dough is left too long in the warm during its second proving, it will tend to collapse. Knock it back and let it rise again if you think it has gone beyond its intended bulk.

Don't leave the rolls on the hot baking tray or the bases will keep on cooking. A wire rack is ideal for cooling them.

MULTIGRAIN BREAD

Brown flours make better loaves than rolls, so shape this dough into cigar-shaped baguettes – I mean fat, expensive cigars, not those unwanted panatellas you got as a Christmas present. Slice the bread at the last moment before serving, after another trip to the oven for reheating.

MAKES 6 SMALL LOAVES

125g (4 1/2oz/1 stick) butter
400ml (14floz/1 3/4 cups)
  milk
1 tablespoon honey
40g (1 1/2oz) fresh yeast
  (1 1/2 x 1oz cakes)
1kg (2lb 4oz) multigrain
  flour such as Granary flour
  (3 cups unbleached
  all-purpose flour + 3 cups
  stoneground wholewheat
  flour + 1 cup malted
  wheat flakes)
2 medium eggs (2 large
  eggs)
1 level tablespoon salt

Melt the butter. Meanwhile, in a separate saucepan, heat 100ml (3 1/2floz/1/2 cup) of the milk to lukewarm. Dissolve the honey in the milk, then mix in the yeast. Leave for 15 minutes, until it bubbles.

Mix the flour, eggs, salt, and melted butter together in a large bowl. Add the yeasty milk, plus all the remaining milk, and mix to a dough. Knead for 10 minutes, then cover with plastic wrap and leave to prove until doubled in bulk.

Knock back the dough and shape into six cigar-like loaves. Lay them on an oiled baking tray and leave to prove. Meanwhile, heat the oven to 220°C (425°F/Gas 7).

When the loaves have doubled in volume they are ready to bake – this should take around 20 minutes depending on their thickness. Tap the bases for the hollow sound that shows they are done. Place on a wire rack or a cool baking tray to cool.

VARIATIONS
For excellent walnut bread to go with cheese, make around half the quantity above and replace the honey with 50g (2oz/1/8 cup) brown sugar. Heat the butter with a sprig of rosemary and add 50g (2oz/1/2 cup) of chopped walnuts to the dry ingredients. Otherwise, proceed in exactly the same manner.

POINTS TO WATCH
This recipe makes quite a large batch, enough for six hungry or 12 small appetites, but the loaves freeze well so any that remain need not be wasted.

BROWN SODA BREAD

Soda bread is like a large savoury scone, and as with scones, the raising agent is sodium bicarbonate, usually in reaction with buttermilk or tartaric acid. The dough for this popular Irish bread contains a mixture of brown and white flours and the proportions are variable. Less brown flour makes a lighter, easier loaf. More brown flour brings more flavour and complexity. In the manner of a professional politician, I have made a decent compromise. It's traditional – in Ireland anyway – to make a round loaf and mark it into quarters, known as farls, with a sharp knife.

MAKES 1 LOAF

350g (12oz) wholemeal flour (3 cups stoneground wholewheat flour)

100g (3 1/2oz) plain white flour (3/4 cup unbleached all-purpose flour), plus extra for dusting

60g (2 1/2oz) oatmeal (1/2 cup briefly processed steel-cut oats)

2 level teaspoons bicarbonate of soda

1 level teaspoon salt

15g (1/2oz/1 tablespoon) softened butter

350ml (12floz/1 1/2 cups) buttermilk, or skimmed milk mixed with 1/2 teaspoon cream of tartar

Heat the oven to 200°C (400°F/Gas 6). In a large bowl, mix together the wholemeal and white flours, oatmeal, bicarbonate of soda and salt. In a jug, combine the soft butter and milk.

Make a well in the centre of the dry ingredients and pour in the liquid, then incorporate the flour bit by bit into the soft dough that forms in the middle.

Knead lightly to make sure everything is well mixed, then shape the dough into a round, flattish loaf. Place on a baking sheet, mark the loaf with a cross and sprinkle it with some extra flour.

Bake for 35-40 minutes. Wrap the loaf loosely with a cloth as it cools if you want a softer crust.

POINTS TO WATCH

Most breadmaking wisdom isn't applicable here. No proving or rising is involved and a lighter touch will be in order.

Buttermilk is a by-product of butter production and bears the same relationship to butter as whey does to cheese. It tastes sharper than milk and is almost fatless. It also can be quite hard to find so some substitute may be needed. Skimmed milk is fine but needs cream of tartar added to do buttermilk's job effectively.

Too much bicarbonate of soda will give an unpleasant aftertaste and, in white soda breads, a strong yellow colour. Don't add extra in the hope of making lighter loaf – it doesn't.

The Merchant House was – and is – a large Jacobean town house backing onto the Corve, the smaller of the town's two rivers. In 1994 a lady and her cat lived in it but wished to sell up and move someplace smaller. The asking price was fair. The ground floor looked more like a restaurant than it does now, but the estate agents were horrified at my casual remark about converting the place and advised their client to sell to another would-be purchaser. They could see problems ahead that might delay their commission, but there wouldn't be any from us – we had fallen for the house and would have as happily just lived in it as work from it, provided I could find some gainful occupation nearby.

My own position was simple. No money, a job as head chef at the estimable Gidleigh Park in Devon which was due to end in a few months, and an unsaleable modern house in a small Dartmoor village near the hotel. My bank account showed a small overdraft and there were no savings to draw on.

A chat with the bank manager produced a plan of action and we were able to buy The Merchant House on the strength of past earnings rather than any optimism of future profits. We took a bridging loan on the Devon property – it took two years to sell – and agreed a personal overdraft and loans which gave us £30,000 to pay for conversions to make the house suitable for use as a restaurant. Easy. The problem, in fact, is not in obtaining the cash for such ventures, but repaying it at some point, for the more you borrow, the shorter time there must be between opening the restaurant and its success. We moved in on Bastille day. All we needed was planning permission.

HONEY BREAD

Each new ingredient added to the basic mixture of flour, yeast and water will affect the bread's texture as well as its flavour. Honey used in any quantity instead of sugar, for instance, tends to give a softer dough so a little more flour is needed to compensate. This recipe is basically a brioche but the substitution of honey for sugar changes its taste significantly. We serve it, toasted, with chicken liver or foie gras pâté. Made with sugar rather than honey, it makes the world's finest french toast if dipped in cream and beaten egg, then fried (page 171).

MAKES 1 LARGE LOAF

110ml (4floz/1/2 cup) milk
90g (3 1/2oz/1/4 cup) honey
20g (3/4oz) fresh yeast
    (3/4 x 1oz cake)
90g (3 1/2oz/7 tablespoons)
    softened butter
4 medium eggs (4 large
    eggs)
1/2 teaspoon salt
600g (1lb5oz) strong white
    flour (4 cups unbleached
    all-purpose flour)

Heat the milk to lukewarm and combine it with the honey. Crumble the yeast into the mixture and leave it to froth up.

Ensure the butter is thoroughly softened, then beat in the eggs and salt. Stir the resulting mixture into the yeasty milk.

Mix in the flour to form a soft dough. Knead it well for a few minutes so that it becomes shiny and smooth.

Refrigerate the dough for 30 minutes then cover with plastic wrap and leave somewhere warm to prove – the customary doubling in bulk is what's needed.

Knock back the risen dough by kneading once or twice. Dust with flour so that it handles more easily, then place the dough in a 1kg (2lb 4oz) loaf tin for its second proving.

Heat the oven to 220°C (425°F/Gas 7). When the loaf has proved, bake for 45 minutes. Turn it out onto a wire rack to cool.

POINTS TO WATCH
Sticky dough, like sticky any-thing, is awkward to handle. An hour in the fridge after mixing will help considerably.

The quantity of egg and butter in the recipe will give the fin-ished loaf a soft texture. This forms part of its appeal but can be altered by a judicious lessen-ing of the butter content.

The temperature of the honey affects its ability to blend with the lukewarm milk. If it is cold or hard, warm it gently before mixing.

If there's no sign of life half an hour after the milk and yeast have been combined, start again with fresh yeast and more careful attention to the milk's temperature.

The butter will not blend with the eggs unless it is quite pliable. If you are short of time, it can be softened by kneading, beating and generally ill-treating it with a wooden spoon.

HAZELNUT AND APRICOT BREAD

MAKES 2 SMALL LOAVES

*15g (1/2oz) fresh yeast
(1/2 x 1oz cake)*

*120ml (41/2floz/1/2 cup)
lukewarm milk*

1 tablespoon honey

*110g (4oz/2/3 cup) ready-
to-eat dried apricots,
roughly chopped*

*140ml (41/2floz/1/2 cup)
boiling water*

*450g (1lb) white bread flour
(3 cups unbleached
all-purpose flour)*

*85g (31/2oz/2/3 cup)
hazelnuts, toasted and
chopped*

1 teaspoon salt

2 tablespoons hazelnut oil

*60g (21/2oz/1/3 cup) rye
flour*

Mix the yeast with the lukewarm milk and honey and leave for 10 minutes to froth up. At the same time, soak the apricots in the boiling water for 10 minutes.

Mix the flour, hazelnuts and salt together in a large bowl. Pour in the yeast mixture, followed by the hazelnut oil and the apricots along with their soaking liquid. Work into a soft dough.

Knead for 10 minutes then leave, covered, with plastic wrap, for 1 to 11/2 hours to prove.

Knock back the risen dough and turn out onto a work surface covered with the rye flour. Divide the dough in half and knead each piece for 1 minute in the rye flour.

Shape into loaves and place into 2 x 450g (1lb) loaf tins. Cover and leave to prove for about 1 hour.

Heat the oven to 220°C (425°F/Gas 7) and bake the loaves for 40 minutes, then turn out onto a wire rack to cool.

BAGELS

These crisp rolls are the main Jewish contribution to our bread basket. They can be sweetened with dried fruit and cinnamon but are more usually savoury, coated with poppy seeds, or served plain and shiny from their swim in the sugared water. Cream cheese and smoked salmon is a traditional filling but they are also good with butter and jam for breakfast. Whatever you fancy, it is important to eat them as soon as possible after making because they turn stale and leathery really fast.

MAKES 12

*175ml (6floz/3/4 cup) tepid
water*

*25g (1oz) fresh yeast
(1 x 1oz cake)*

4 tablespoons sugar

4 tablespoons vegetable oil

1 level tablespoon salt

*2 medium eggs (2 large
eggs), plus 1 beaten egg
for glazing*

*450g (1lb) strong flour
(32/3 cups unbleached
all-purpose flour)*

Mix the water, yeast and 1/4 tablespoon of the sugar together. Let stand for 10 minutes, by which time it should start to bubble.

Add another 3/4 tablespoon of sugar to the mixture, along with the oil, salt and two of the eggs.

Stir in half the flour, then slowly add the remainder. As the dough becomes difficult to stir, use your hands.

Knead the dough for about 10 minutes so that it is smooth, then cover and leave for around 1 hour to prove.

Knock back the dough by kneading once or twice, then shape into bagels. This is how you do it: divide the dough into 12 equal pieces and roll each into a ball. Flatten the balls with the palm of your hand and then push a hole through the centre of each with a floured finger. Alternatively, you can roll each ball into a cigar shape and join the ends. Cover and leave for 15 minutes.

Heat the oven to 200°C (400°F/Gas 6). In a large pan, bring 2 litres (3 pints 10floz/21/4 quarts) of water to the boil with the remaining 3 tablespoons of sugar.

Drop in the bagels, 3 or 4 at a time. Let them boil for 1 minute, then lift them out with a slotted spoon.

Transfer the bagels to a baking sheet, brush lightly with the beaten egg and bake for 20 minutes or until golden.

POINTS TO WATCH

The preparation method for bagels is rather unusual. They are boiled in slightly sugared water before baking. This boiling completes the proving process so the dough will not need the customary doubling in bulk.

The doughnut-shaped holes tend to heal up as the bagels are brought to the boil. This is one of the occasions in life where a poke with a sharp stick is in order, failing which a little jiggling with the handle of a wooden spoon should put things right.

Remember that batches of flour vary slightly and some absorb more liquid than others. Don't worry if you cannot quite work in all the flour given here.

Stocks, sauces and soups

Stocks and sauces are at the heart of European restaurant food and ought to be the trump card which makes the investment in a meal worthwhile. Classical and provincial French cooking both work on a system whereby a dish can be broken down into components and put together again so that all the people sitting at a table can eat different items freshly cooked and served at the same time. Any piece of meat that takes longer than 20 minutes to cook, such as roast beef or duck, is best done in the home kitchen. Chefs however need to be able to cook meat quickly and the long, slow cooking of bones and trimmings into stocks and sauces can provide the intense flavours that are missing from a rare lamb chop or sirloin steak.

There are basically two types of sauce: gravy and relish. That is, there are those which derive from the meat or fish and are stock-based, and those that provide contrast in the way that a chutney or mustard might. Stock-based sauces need advance preparation. The basic stocks freeze well if you have room. When reduced to a solid jelly, they will keep for a long period but when kept liquid they need to be reboiled each day. Stock is an ideal vehicle for using up trimmings. It is not, however, a substitute for the garbage and should not contain leftovers irrelevant to the flavour wanted. Chicken and fish stocks are both very simple to make; they are not time consuming and do not require many pans. Veal stock is far more complex to do properly at home and ought to be better made in a restaurant, yet I am astounded by the number of keen dinner party cooks who make it at home and keep it in the freezer.

The making of soups and sauces are related skills. Sauces are always used in smallish quantities and in conjunction with a portion of meat, fish or vegetables so the volume of flavouring has to be turned up sufficiently to be effective. Remember when tasting soup for seasoning that the same rules do not apply and salt and spice levels have to reflect the fact that a bowlful rather than a tablespoonful will be eaten.

There are basically two types of sauce: gravy and relish.

Soups are generally not popular in restaurants. People do not seem to feel as though they are getting their money's worth if they do not have something solid as a starter. Sweet soups, however, are coming into vogue now as puddings. I find them curiously unappealing, the best ones being a reworking of traditional ideas with slightly varying volumes of sauce to solid. A summer berry soup with warm macaroons and plenty of fresh raspberries and redcurrants would be fine; praline and chocolate soups however strike me as being like bedtime drinks for those who have not yet discovered hard liquor.

CHICKEN STOCK

White chicken stock is made by simmering bones and water together for 40 minutes. Dark chicken stock, which is my preference, involves roasting or frying the bones before boiling and gives a more pronounced flavour, in the same way as a roast chicken tastes more distinctive than one that's been boiled. All poached and roasted foods differ for the same reason. Complex changes happen at temperatures over 150°C/300°F/Gas 2. These are called Maillard reactions and involve proteins on the outside of the food caramelizing into richer as well as darker flavours. The effect is caused by the temperatures reached and not just the length of time spent cooking the bones.

MAKES 1.5 LITRES
(2 1/2 PINTS/6 1/4 CUPS)

3 whole chicken carcasses,
*   or 750g (1lb 10oz)*
*   winglets, necks and*
*   gizzards*
1 onion, chopped
1 leek, chopped
1 small carrot, chopped

Roast the chicken bones at 200°C/400°F/Gas 6 for around 30 minutes or until lightly browned.

Transfer the roast bones to a stockpot or large saucepan. Drain off any fat from the roasting tin, then deglaze it by pouring in 225ml (8floz/1 cup) of cold water. Bring the water to the boil, scraping up as much of the caramelized cooking juices as possible, then add to the pot of bones.

Pour in 2.25 litres (4 pints/10 1/4 cups) of water and bring the pot to the boil. Skim off the foam that rises to the surface of the stock, then add the chopped vegetables. Return to the boil and simmer for 1 1/2 hours. Should the water level drop below that of the chicken during simmering, top it up.

Strain the stock and leave to cool completely. Refrigerate the stock as soon as it is cool. The fat will then rise to the surface and solidify, albeit softly. It will skim off easily.

POINTS TO WATCH

A golden brown is the objective when roasting the carcasses. Charred and burnt ingredients will give lots of colour but also an unpleasant bitter note.

For a more concentrated flavour, add more carcasses or giblets rather than keep the stock boiling for ages. The chicken will give up all its flavour within 2 hours and no improvement is made by longer cooking.

Clear, clean stock has no grease or fat. Most fat will rise to the top as the stock cools and can be skimmed off then. If the stock boils too hard during cooking, some of the fat will emulsify into the stock making it look cloudy and taste greasy. Aim for gentle simmering.

When deglazing a pan, the idea is to incorporate any residue stuck to the base of the tin into liquid, the same as in making gravy. To do it, bring the liquid to the boil and use a wooden spoon to scrape up as much residue as possible.

FISH STOCK

Restraint is the key to this recipe. The stock cooks only 30 minutes and care spent on it will repay you with clear, well-flavoured soups and sauces. Fish bones for stock are usually free and vary in suitability. Haddock, hake, halibut, monk, sole, turbot and whiting are good. Mediocre results will be obtained from bass, mullet, plaice and salmon, while herring, mackerel and other oily fish are poor choices.

MAKES 1.5 LITRES
(2 1/2 PINTS/6 1/4 CUPS)
1.5kg (3lb 6oz) fish bones
25g (1oz/1/4 stick) butter
1 medium leek, chopped
1 onion, chopped
250ml (9floz/1 cup) dry
  white wine
a few peppercorns

Wash the bones in cold water and remove any traces of blood. Cut the bones into manageable lengths.

Melt the butter in a large saucepan or stock pot and gently fry the chopped vegetables. Add the fish bones and cook for 3-4 minutes, turning them over, until they no longer smell raw.

Pour on the wine, then add 2 litres (3 1/2 pints/8 3/4 cups) of water and the peppercorns. Bring to a gentle boil and simmer for 30 minutes. Remove from the heat and allow the stock to settle for a further 10 minutes before straining.

VARIATIONS
The main variant is shellfish stock, which obviously calls for shellfish, and whole shell-on prawns or shrimp are ideal used in conjunction with the fish bones mentioned. Usually some stronger ingredient like tomato passata (sieved tomatoes) or chilli is added.

Mussels produce wonderful stock, good for soup and sauces alike. Follow the recipe above but fry the chopped onion before adding mussels rather than fish bones, then some white wine and water. You can eat the cooked mussels with a little salad dressing later.

POINTS TO WATCH
The bones should cook gently and without colouring in a little butter or oil before any water is added. This develops the flavour in the same way as roasting chicken or veal bones for meat stocks.

Avoid powerful flavourings like celery, or at least use them sparingly. The delicate flavour of fish bones cannot compete with them in the way roast veal bones can and your stock may turn into a fishy tasting celery broth.

Do not add salt to this or any other stock. Remember: stock is a component, not a finished dish.

To achieve greater concentration of flavour, either increase the ratio of bones to water or, once the stock is cooked and strained, reduce the volume of stock by extra boiling.

After you have strained the stock, let the debris cool before wrapping and consignment to the garbage. The combination of heat and spiky bones is lethal to plastic refuse bags.

VEAL STOCK AND DEMI-GLACE

Demi-glace acquired a bad image when Escoffier-style cooking was replaced by nouvelle cuisine. In the hands of poor cooks it had become a byword for all the flour-heavy, all-purpose brown sauces used to coat chops and steaks. The word jus replaced it, implying that no flour is used. Really gelatinous veal bones may be able to thicken stock sufficiently with no flour at all, but in my experience two or three tablespoons of flour, cooked out thoroughly in the liquid, will help the texture quite a bit.

Veal stock and demi-glace are time consuming and not worth making in small quantities. Demi-glace is made over three days, although there is very little work involved, and the stock requires occasional rather than constant attention as it reduces.

FOR THE STOCK

**MAKES 3 LITRES
(5 PINTS/12 1/2 CUPS)**

3kg (6lb 11oz) veal bones

*500g (1lb 2oz) onions,
roughly chopped*

*300g (10 1/2oz) celery,
roughly chopped*

*200g (7oz) leeks, roughly
chopped*

*200g (7oz) carrots, roughly
chopped*

FOR THE DEMI-GLACE

**MAKES 2 LITRES
(3 1/2 PINTS/8 3/4 CUPS)**

*3 litres (5 pints/12 1/2 cups)
veal stock (above)*

3 tablespoons olive oil

*200g (7oz) onions, roughly
chopped*

*200g (7oz) carrots, roughly
chopped*

*200g (7oz) leeks, roughly
chopped*

2 cloves garlic, chopped

*1kg (2lb 4oz) shin of beef,
diced*

*3 tablespoons plain
(all-purpose) flour*

*3 tablespoons tomato
passata (sieved tomatoes)*

1/2 bottle red wine

To make the stock, roast the bones at 200°C/400°F/Gas 6 for around 30 minutes or until browned.

Transfer the bones to a large stock pot and cover with 5 litres (7 1/2 pints/4 1/2 quarts) of cold water. Bring the pot to the boil, skim off any foam, then add the chopped vegetables. Simmer for 8 hours, topping up the water levels and skimming as necessary. Strain into a bucket or similar-sized container.

To make the demi-glace, bring the prepared veal stock to the boil, skim then reduce the heat to a gentle simmer.

Heat 1 tablespoon of the olive oil in a large frying pan or wok and fry one-third of the chopped vegetables and garlic until they start to colour. Add one-third of the diced shin and continue to fry, at a high heat, until this too browns.

Stir in 1 tablespoon of flour and continue to cook for a few minutes before adding 1 tablespoon of tomato passata and one-third of the red wine. Stir until the liquid is smooth.

Add the contents of the frying pan to the simmering stock. Repeat the process twice with the remaining ingredients.

Simmer for 4 hours, topping up the liquid level occasionally with cold water and skimming away any foam or grease that rises to the surface. Strain into a bucket or other large container. Leave to cool, then refrigerate overnight.

Next day, remove any fat from the surface, transfer the mixture to a pot and bring to the boil. Simmer for a further 2 hours. As the liquid level reduces, add a little cold water and skim off any grease that rises to the surface. It is then ready to use.

POINTS TO WATCH

The correct cooking time for the bones will vary with their size. Roast them until they are brown but not black.

HOLLANDAISE SAUCE

Hollandaise is a warm emulsion of cooked egg yolk and melted butter, rather like a hot version of mayonnaise. It's one of the few buttery sauces that can be served with fried food and, if you get it right, you can tailor it to your heart's content with additional flavourings.

FOR 4 PERSONS

200g (7oz/1 3/4 sticks)
    butter
3 egg yolks
50ml (2floz/1/4 cup)
    white wine
1 teaspoon lemon juice
a dash of Tabasco sauce or
    cayenne pepper
salt

Clarify the butter by heating it slowly in a small saucepan.

Whisk the egg yolks and white wine together over a low heat until thick like a cooked sabayon.

Remove from the heat and gradually whisk in the butter oil, adding a spoonful at a time. Finally, whisk in the lemon juice, Tabasco sauce or cayenne and season with salt.

VARIATIONS

Mint and thyme are common flavourings. Otherwise, I tend to leave it be, but you can also add saffron or ground almonds.

POINTS TO WATCH

As with mayonnaise, hollandaise is most liable to split because of overthickening or adding too high a proportion of butter to other liquid. Have a little wine or hot water ready nearby to put things right if needed.

When clarifying butter, the idea is that the oil in the butter separates and rises to the top. If it gets too hot, allow it to cool slightly or it may spoil the sauce.

When whisking the yolks and wine it is best to use a pan with a rounded bottom rather than straight edges because the yolks will tend to coagulate into scrambled eggs in the corners. If you have nothing suitable, make the sauce in a heatproof bowl suspended over a pan of hot water.

WATERCRESS SAUCE

The astringency of watercress makes for a good sauce. This is designed to partner veal, poultry or offal. To serve alongside fish, salmon for instance, you need only substitute fish stock for the demi-glace.

FOR 4 PERSONS
a small bunch of watercress
2 tablespoons dry vermouth
1 small shallot
4 tablespoons demi-glace
   (page 31)
2 tablespoons double
   (heavy) cream
a few drops of lemon juice
salt and pepper

Pick off any hairy stems from the watercress and coarsely chop the remaining stems and leaves. Chop the shallot.

Heat the vermouth and shallot in a small saucepan until just boiling, then add the demi-glace and cream. Stir in the watercress.

Add a little lemon juice and taste to check the balance of the seasoning. Bring the sauce to the boil, then serve.

POINTS TO WATCH
Like basil and parsley, watercress loses both freshness and colour if kept for too long in hot liquid. It does, however, need a short burst of heat to move the flavour on from raw to cooked. Adding the watercress about a minute before serving is ideal.

RED PEPPER SAUCE

Delicious with white fish such as monk or cod, this sauce can also be served with chicken or white meat provided the fish stock is replaced with chicken stock.

FOR 4 PERSONS
1 large red bell pepper
2 shallots
1 tablespoon olive oil
200ml (7floz/scant 1 cup)
fish stock (page 29)
2 tablespoons dry vermouth
1 tablespoon lemon juice
4 dashes Tabasco sauce
salt and pepper

Deseed and slice the bell pepper. Roughly chop the shallots. In a saucepan, gently stew the bell pepper and shallots in the olive oil until tender.

Add the stock and vermouth to the vegetables. Cover the pan and cook gently for about 20 minutes.

Purée the mixture in a blender with the lemon juice, Tabasco sauce and salt and pepper to taste.

POINTS TO WATCH
Be sure to season the sauce well, otherwise it can taste like canned tomato soup.

If you want a thicker sauce, blend in another tablespoon of olive oil rather than using any cream or butter to thicken.

FRESH GINGER, GARLIC AND TOMATO SAUCE

Not a sauce from the classic repertoire, this salsa-like mixture goes well with any slightly oily fish such as red mullet or sea bass. It is also a fine accompaniment to vegetable dishes such as stuffed aubergine (eggplant) or courgette (zucchini).

FOR 4 PERSONS

4 large tomatoes
10cm (4in) piece fresh
  ginger
2 shallots
2 large cloves garlic
1 small red chilli
1 tablespoon light sesame
  or sunflower oil
1 tablespoon tomato
  passata (sieved tomatoes)
25g (1oz/1/4 stick)
  unsalted butter
1 tablespoon chopped
  coriander (cilantro)
1 tablespoon chopped chives
salt and black pepper

Skin and deseed the tomatoes and dice the flesh. Peel and finely chop the ginger, shallots and garlic. Finely chop the chilli.

In a saucepan, sweat the ginger, shallot, garlic and chilli in the oil. Add the passata and 1 tablespoon of water and cook gently for 2 minutes. Add the diced tomato, some salt and milled black pepper, and allow to heat through.

Just before serving, heat the sauce with the butter and chopped herbs, stirring or whisking so that the butter thickens the sauce.

POINTS TO WATCH
After the diced tomato, salt and pepper have been added to the pan, the mixture can be cooled and kept in the fridge until needed.

The joy of opening a restaurant lies in the planning. The earnest conversation of the early days, well lubricated by wine and optimism, concentrates on lofty matters of policy and pricing, which sort of tables and chairs to buy, tablecloths or no tablecloths, which design of crockery, all that sort of thing. Nearer the time it takes a turn for the worse.

Having borrowed money and installed ourselves, we applied for planning consent. A local architect had drawn up some plans that covered the main concerns of the chief planning officer and the council building supervisor. They were a nightmare. A house with two bathrooms and four lavatories needed another place to pee in. A staircase had to be re-routed, leaving our bedroom as the only corridor to the loft conversion. Expensive emergency lighting and fire precautions had to be installed. Worst of all, a new front door was to be carved into the front of the house and this would need permission from English Heritage.

The local paper gave our proposed venture front page headlines: 'Television chef upsets local residents with restaurant scheme'. Having done hardly any television, except in the West Country, I was flattered and

Anja amused at the elevation to celebrity status. However, the petition against our plan from disgruntled neighbours with parking and noise worries was more disturbing. We followed the to and fro of correspondence in the papers with interest but didn't join in. The sewers wouldn't cope, property prices would fall, the four horsemen of the apocalypse would ride through Ludlow spreading gloom and despond. Permission was eventually granted, with the proviso that we cannot serve takeaway meals. We were nonetheless grateful and the builders moved in forthwith.

Having building work done is stressful. Your house is a site, not a home, and things that should be funny take on a surreal and paranoia-inducing aspect. The building supervisor noticed one day that some bedroom windows that have served well since Oliver Cromwell rode past were too small to comply with fire regulations. What to do? Murder seemed a more uplifting prospect than suicide, but Anja found a solution: we would not call that room a bedroom, we would call it a lobby, in which case the windows would be fine. Everyone is content and we have slept in the upstairs lobby ever since.

NORTH SEA FISH SOUP

Most fish soups have great-tasting broth, but also seafood pieces with a lousy texture. Prolonged cooking does no favours to seafood. This recipe has the freshness and immediacy of just-cooked fish and, in order to succeed, must be made only just before needed. The selection of seafood given here is a guideline only – it is the technique that produces the dish and within reason, the more types and textures of fish you can use in this soup, the better.

FOR 4 PERSONS

FOR THE SOUP

*500g (1lb 2oz) mixed fish
fillets and shellfish, such
as cod, sea bass, red
mullet and scallops*

*600ml (21floz/2⅔ cups)
chicken stock*

4 tablespoons white wine

2 shallots, chopped

the juice of ½ lemon

1 egg yolk

*1 tablespoon double
(heavy) cream*

*50g (2oz/½ cup) cooked
whole prawns, shelled*

*1 tomato, peeled, deseeded
and chopped*

*1 tablespoon chopped
parsley*

FOR THE CROÛTONS

1 slice white bread

a little olive oil, for frying

To make the croûtons, dice the bread and fry the cubes in the olive oil until golden. Set aside until needed.

Cut the mixed fish and shellfish (not the prawns) into chunks. Meanwhile, bring the stock, white wine and shallots to the boil in a soup pot.

Season the fish and shellfish with lemon juice, salt and pepper, then add them to the pot in the order in which they take to cook – bass first, then cod and mullet and, lastly, scallops.

In a small bowl, stir the egg yolk and cream together. Turn off the direct heat under the soup and whisk in the cream mixture.

Stir in the prawns, chopped tomato and parsley, and finally the croûtons. Serve the soup immediately.

POINTS TO WATCH

Some fish cook more quickly than others. In order that they all arrive at the finishing line simultaneously, you must either cut the denser fish into smaller pieces than the others, or put them in the stock a little earlier.

Chicken stock is marginally better than fish stock for this soup as it has more body. It will taste fishy enough once the ingredients are cooked in it.

PHEASANT AND CHESTNUT SOUP

A degree of sweetness compliments gamey flavours. Even a few unsweetened chestnuts will give this to the soup. For this recipe you could use roasted shelled fresh chestnuts or those from a can. The quantity given here will provide four people with lunch or six with a substantial starter.

FOR 4 – 6 PERSONS

1 pheasant
1 medium carrot
1 onion
1 clove garlic
a small knob of fresh ginger
a little oil or butter, for frying
1 teaspoon ground cinnamon
1 teaspoon ground coriander
1 teaspoon ground cumin
1 teaspoon grated nutmeg
1.5 litres (2 1/2 pints/6 1/4 cups) chicken stock
25g (1oz/1/4 cup) cooked chestnuts
1 tablespoon lemon juice
1 tablespoon double (heavy) cream
a few coriander (cilantro) or flat-leaf parsley leaves, to garnish
salt and pepper

Take the pheasant meat off the bones. Peel and chop the carrot, onion, garlic and ginger and fry in a little oil or butter with the leg meat from the pheasant until the mixture starts to brown.

Add the spices and continue frying for a few moments. Add the stock and bring to the boil, then add the chestnuts and leave to simmer for 30 minutes.

Add the pieces of breast meat from the pheasant and continue simmering for about 20 minutes or until the pheasant is just done. Lift the breast from the soup and cut it into large dice.

Purée the soup in a blender, then pass through a sieve. Return the soup to the pan and reheat. Add the diced pheasant breast, then the lemon juice and cream. Season to taste, garnish with the coriander or parsley leaves and serve.

POINTS TO WATCH

The spices used in this soup are aromatic rather than hot. The mixture therefore needs a few drops of lemon juice to balance the flavour, otherwise it will be too akaline-tasting.

SAFFRON AND LEMON SOUP

This was a regular menu item at Robert Carrier's restaurant in Islington in the early 1970s. In those days we used stock cubes and water rather than stock, but it still seemed to taste okay.

FOR 4 PERSONS

250g (9oz) leeks
150g (5oz) potatoes
1 tablespoon olive oil
1 small onion, chopped
1 teaspoon saffron threads
1 litre (1 3/4 pints/4 1/2 cups)
  chicken stock (page 28)
4 teaspoons white wine
4 tablespoons cream
1 lemon
chopped chives, to garnish
salt and pepper

Wash the leeks and cut them into 3cm (1 1/4in) pieces. Peel the potatoes and cut them into cubes the same size as the leeks.

Heat the oil in a large saucepan and sweat the onion. Add the leeks, potato and saffron. Pour on the stock and bring to the boil. Cover and simmer for 20 minutes until the potatoes are done.

Purée the soup in a blender, then return to the pan. Stir in the white wine and half the cream. Season to taste.

To finish, acidulate the remaining cream with a few drops of lemon juice. Cut four slices from the lemon and spread the cream over each slice. Place the soup in serving bowls, float the lemon slices on top and sprinkle with chives.

POINTS TO WATCH

The soup is ready for blending and serving when the potatoes are soft. Any further cooking will harm the soup's texture.

PARSNIP AND SHERRY SOUP WITH HAZELNUT PESTO

Strangely, the pleasure of crisp, sweet roast parsnips is little known among the gastronomically inclined French, who consider the parsnip to be animal feed – their loss, of course. Parsnips were one of the few foodstuffs exported from Britain during Roman times. The emperor Tiberius evidently liked them but sadly only in the belief that they were some form of aphrodisiac. Presumably it was the shape and sturdiness rather than the flavour or nutritional qualities that appealed to him. No matter, they taste wonderful. Parsnip soup works well with a little dry sherry. The addition of hazelnut pesto, which I came across in an American food magazine some years ago, gives both contrast and lift to the dish.

FOR 4 – 6 PERSONS

FOR THE SOUP

100g (3 1/2oz/7 tablespoons)
  unsalted butter
500g (1lb 2oz) parsnips,
  peeled and chopped
4 shallots, chopped
3 small leeks, white and
  pale green parts only,
  chopped
4 tablespoons dry sherry
2 tablespoons double
  (heavy) cream
salt and pepper

FOR THE PESTO

75g (3oz/heaped 1/2 cup)
  toasted hazelnuts
a small bunch of flat-leaf
  parsley
2 cloves garlic
3 tablespoons olive oil
1 tablespoon hazelnut oil

Blend all the pesto ingredients together using a food processor, blender or pestle and mortar. Refrigerate until needed.

To make the soup, heat the butter in a heavy pot and cook the parsnips, shallots and leeks until brown.

Add the sherry and boil until it has evaporated. Stir in 750ml (1 pint 6floz/3 1/4 cups) of water and bring the soup to the boil. Cover and simmer for 20 minutes, by which time the vegetables should be quite soft.

Purée the soup in batches using a food processor or blender, then return it to the pot and reheat adding the cream. Taste to test the seasoning and add salt and pepper as needed.

Serve with a spoonful of the hazelnut pesto in each bowl.

POINTS TO WATCH

Parsnips need to be caramelized to be at their best and sweetest.

If you are using a food processor or blender rather than a pestle and mortar to mix the pesto, it is easier to make if the quantity given here is doubled. The remaining pesto keeps and freezes well and can be served with pasta or as a sauce for grilled meat and fish.

Starters, salads and dressings

Cold starters make sense from the organizational point of view. Large kitchens have a separate section to handle cold starters and people giving dinner parties at home like the idea of having something sitting ready in the fridge to serve. I don't like anything, other than ice cream, to look or taste as if it recently occupied shelf space in the refrigerator and the differences between home and commercial cooking here work to the professional chef's advantage. As you don't have to sit and eat with anyone, or pretend that things are running smoothly when they are not, you can dress salads and compile starters as near to the time of their consumption as possible.

A starter is not just a small course that you have before the main dish of meat or fish. It has a distinct function in the meal and should stimulate rather than satisfy. The level and style of seasoning can be stronger in the starter than in the main course because the quantity of food is smaller. A small portion of roast beef and Yorkshire pudding served first would always seem like a sawn-off main course, whereas some cold roast beef served in a vegetable salad dressed with a highly-flavoured vinaigrette or sauce is fine. Most successful starters make good sandwich fillings, though fish regularly fits the bill too, partly because it is

Dress salads as near to the time of their consumption as possible.

light but mostly because the treatments based on lemon or white wine that are regularly used for fish suit the moment. It is the acidity of the dressing, or a fresh-tasting style of sauce, in a cold starter that makes the dish work at this particular point in the meal.

The definition of a salad is quite hazy. 'Anything with a salad dressing' is probably the answer and most cold starters fall into this category. Exceptions such as fruit (melon for example) qualify because, when in perfect condition, they have a natural balance of sweetness and acidity that dressings hope to equal. Top quality oil, extra virgin olive or walnut perhaps, needs nothing other than a little salt to dress salad. However most salads are interesting as a result of the skilled blending of oil, vinegar or lemon, and seasonings.

Good hot starters can be small portions of risotto or pasta with a piquant sauce, warm fish dishes, or even some elaborate vegetable confection. The first course is less likely to feature red meat served hot as this will usually figure later in the meal and what's needed is the semblance of orderly progression from light to heavier dishes. In grand meals with several courses, and where a cold hors d'oeuvre has already been offered, a change of style and pace will be needed for the next small course.

VINAIGRETTE

It is the mustard that turns a vinaigrette into a creamy emulsion, but if you don't want the flavour of mustard in your dressing, measure the other ingredients given here and whisk them together just before the salad is to be tossed and served. The dressing will soon separate back into a base of vinegar and seasoning under a pool of oil and should be whisked just before each further use.

FOR 4 PORTIONS

1 tablespoon Dijon mustard
1 tablespoon white wine
*   vinegar*
50ml (2floz/1/4 cup)
*   sunflower oil*
50ml (2floz/1/4 cup) olive oil
salt and pepper

Stir the mustard and vinegar together, then season with salt and pepper. Whisk in the oil, drop by drop.

VARIATIONS

Any change in the type of vinegar or oil will completely change the flavour of the dressing. A few sprigs of thyme and some chopped toasted pine nuts will convert this vinaigrette into something more substantial that can be used in a salad with roast game or hot chicken livers. Chopped shallot, capers and chopped parsley used here will give a dressing to partner warm veal or white offal such as brains and sweetbreads.

POINTS TO WATCH
Stronger is not necessarily better with oil or vinegar. Look for balance in the final dressing and don't hesitate to mix vegetable oil with olive or walnut oil, or plain wine vinegar with sherry vinegar if that's what is needed.

SALAD CREAM

Not to be confused with the over-sweet commercial product, salad cream has, since the post-war years of my childhood, moved from being the only help available to those eating a plateful of rabbit food to a position where it is largely ignored as an option. Properly made, it has possibilities.

FOR 4 PORTIONS

2 hard-boiled eggs
1 teaspoon Dijon mustard
1 teaspoon caster
*   (granulated) sugar*
a pinch of cayenne pepper
150ml (5floz/10 table
*   spoons) double (heavy)*
*   cream*
1 tablespoon lemon juice
salt and pepper

Separate the hard-boiled eggs into whites and yolks. Chop the whites and keep to one side to mix into the dressing later.

Make a paste of the yolks with 1 teaspoon of water, plus the mustard, sugar, cayenne and some salt and pepper.

To incorporate the cream, trickle it onto the paste while whisking or stirring. Add the lemon juice.

Adjust the seasoning to taste and stir in the chopped egg white.

VARIATIONS
The sauce can be made sweeter or sharper by adjusting the amounts of lemon and sugar used. Chopped herbs and anchovy essence make good additions.

POINTS TO WATCH
The process of acidulating cream by adding lemon juice has the effect of stiffening and thickening the cream. It looks attractive in a bowl or sauceboat but like any other dressing it is best tossed with the other ingredients so that all are coated equally.

MAYONNAISE

The Californian food scientist Harold McGee, author of *On Food and Cooking* and, to my mind, as influential a writer as Elizabeth David, has experimented on mayonnaise to discover just how much oil and egg yolk can emulsify. The answer was gallons, so it is the ratio of liquid to oil that is crucial when it comes to successful blending of mayonnaise. That and the flavour of course.

FOR 4 PORTIONS

3 egg yolks
1 teaspoon Dijon mustard
2 tablespoons white wine
  vinegar
a few drops of
  Worcestershire sauce
300ml (11floz/1 1/3 cups)
  sunflower oil
salt and pepper

Whisk together the egg yolks, mustard and seasoning. Whisk in the oil, initially drop by drop, then as the emulsion becomes stronger, add it more quickly.

VARIATIONS

Thousands. Crushed garlic or almost any herb can be included. Tartare sauce is made by adding chopped gherkin, capers and parsley. Cocktail sauce – the sweetish pink gunk that usually coats prawn cocktails – is mayonnaise with tomato ketchup and a little extra Worcestershire sauce.

POINTS TO WATCH

Once you have measured the relative quantities of oil to egg and vinegar, stick to them. Alter the ratio only if you feel the mayonnaise should be more or less sharp. Tap water will thin it without altering the flavour if that's all that's needed.

The ingredients are affected by temperature. Cold ingredients emulsify less easily so try to have them all at room temperature.

Curdled mayonnaise can often be rectified by whisking in some warm water or vinegar. If you have a complete disaster on your hands and are beginning to feel depressed, pour the mixture into a blender, add warm water or vinegar, and whizz until smooth.

Mustard is not essential to this process should the flavour disagree, however it does help to emulsify the sauce. Milder or stronger mustards can be substituted for Dijon. However, olive oil used on its own does not make good mayonnaise, so always use some sunflower oil.

RED PEPPER BAVAROIS WITH ASPARAGUS

FOR 4 PERSONS

20 asparagus spears
a little olive oil
salt and black pepper

FOR THE BAVAROIS

3 large red bell peppers
1 tablespoon lemon juice
1 teaspoon caster
  (granulated) sugar
6 drops Tabasco sauce
1 tablespoon olive oil
250g (9oz/1 heaping cup)
  mascarpone cheese

First make the bavarois. Peel the bell peppers. Cut one into very fine dice. Place in a small bowl with half the lemon juice, plus the sugar and 2 drops of Tabasco sauce. Leave to marinate.

Cut the other two bell peppers into chunks. Purée them in a blender with the remaining lemon juice, 4 drops of Tabasco sauce, the olive oil and some black pepper.

Add the mascarpone to the blender and process again. Scrape the mixture into a bowl and add the finely chopped bell pepper and its marinade. Leave in the fridge until set.

Drop the asparagus into a pan of salted boiling water to cook for 2 to 3 minutes, depending on the thickness of the spears. Drain and refresh in cold water.

Dry the asparagus, season with salt and pepper then brush with olive oil. Use 2 tablespoons dipped in warm water to shape the bavarois mixture into quenelles and lay the aparagus alongside.

POINTS TO WATCH

Peel the bell peppers with a vegetable peeler rather than by scorching and scraping. This retains the fresh raw taste.

Refrigeration is important in this recipe because it will take 2 to 3 hours for the bavarois mixture to set well enough to be shaped into quenelles. However, you could serve the mixture in ramekins instead.

SCALLOP TARTARE

FOR 4 PERSONS

12 large scallops,
  white part only
2 medium potatoes
oil, for shallow frying
1 tablespoon lime juice
1 teaspoon soy sauce
6 drops Tabasco sauce or
  similar chilli sauce
4 teaspoons crème fraîche
4 teaspoons caviar
1 tablespoon chopped chives
1 tablespoon chopped raw
  carrot
salt and black pepper

Finely chop the white scallop meat, place in a bowl and chill.

Boil the potatoes for 4 minutes in their jackets. Cool, then peel and coarsely grate. Shape into 8 small röstis and shallow-fry in hot oil until crisp and brown. Keep warm until needed.

Just before serving, mix the lime juice, soy and Tabasco sauces and some salt and pepper into the scallop meat.

Spread the mixture along the centre of chilled serving plates, then add a teaspoon of crème fraîche and a teaspoon of caviar to each. Sprinkle with the chopped chives and raw carrot and serve with the potato röstis.

POINTS TO WATCH

Frozen scallops will not do. They will have been soaked before freezing and will be swollen with water. This makes them look bigger but the frozen water tears the delicate texture and they will have a tired and defeated look when defrosted.

Only the white part is needed so choose those scallops that don't have huge corals.

Keep the chopped scallops as cold as possible without letting them freeze and only add the lime juice and seasonings at the very last moment, as they will start to 'cook' the scallops.

GRILLED COD WITH BITTER SALAD LEAVES AND PARSLEY DRESSING

This treatment suits any grilled white fish and, if money is no object, Dover sole fillets look elegant served this way. The dressing is similar to pesto, but with the addition of stock or wine and lemon juice. The result looks rather like avocado purée but acts as sauce for the fish and a dressing for the leaves.

FOR 4 PERSONS

4 cod fillets, 100g (3 1/2oz)
  each

about 1 tablespoon olive oil

a selection of bitter leaves
  including belgian endive,
  corn salad and frisée

2 tomatoes, skinned, seeded
  and diced

1/2 lemon

FOR THE DRESSING

120ml (4floz/1/2 cup) olive
  oil

100g (3 1/2oz/5 cups lightly
  packed) flat-leaf parsley

1 shallot, chopped

4 tablespoons fish stock,

1 tablespoon pine nuts

1 tablespoon lemon juice

1 sprig basil

1 clove garlic, chopped

a dash of Tabasco sauce

salt and black pepper

To make the dressing, process all the ingredients in a blender (a food processor won't do). It will form a thick purée and will set fairly solid if kept in the refrigerator.

Brush the fish fillets with olive oil, season lightly and grill or broil them. Combine the salad leaves and tomatoes and arrange them round the edges of the serving plates. Sprinkle with a few drops of olive oil and some salt.

Put a spoonful of parsley dressing at the centre of each plate and lay the cooked fish fillets on top. Squeeze a little lemon juice over each fillet before serving.

POINTS TO WATCH

The ratio of salad leaves to fish is easily misunderstood. The leaves are scattered round the edge of the plate so that the dressing can rest in the centre with the fish placed on top. Anything put in the centre of a plate appears larger, and anything around the rim less, so here the salad leaves will appear less than in reality. Make the salad first in the middle of the plate. Assess the quantity in relation to the piece of fish, then move the salad out to the edge of the plate.

PIKE QUENELLES WITH SHRIMP AND DILL

It is a triumph that someone came up with the idea of using pike as a quenelle. It is ideal for the purpose, the dryness allowing for the incorporation of large amounts of egg and cream, and the array of small irritating bones are sieved out before cooking.

FOR 4 PERSONS

FOR THE QUENELLES

300g (10 1/2oz) pike fillet

3 egg whites

300ml (11floz/1 1/3 cups)
*   double (heavy) cream*

a little grated nutmeg

25g (1oz/1/4 stick) butter

salt and pepper

FOR THE SAUCE

100g (3 1/2oz/1 scant cup)
*   shrimp or prawns*

1 tablespoon Irish whiskey

50ml (2floz/1/4 cup) white
*   wine*

1 shallot, chopped

100g (3 1/2oz/7 tablespoons)
*   unsalted butter, cubed*

1 tablespoon crème fraîche

2 tablespoons dill, roughly
*   chopped*

a few drops of lemon juice

Macerate the shrimps in the whiskey for 1 hour.

Cut the pike fillet into small pieces, then chop in a food processor. Add the egg whites one by one, processing until smooth.

Chill the mixture over a bowl of iced water. Beat in the cream, a level teaspoon of salt, some pepper and a little grated nutmeg.

Pipe the quenelle mixture into four sausage shapes onto pieces of plastic wrap. Wrap carefully and chill.

Poach the wrapped quenelles in hot but not boiling water for around 20 minutes or until they are cooked through.

To make the sauce, in a small pan, boil the wine and shallot together until the volume has reduced by half. Whisk in the butter, a piece at a time, then add the crème fraîche, dill and macerated shrimps. Taste and add lemon juice as necessary.

Heat the butter for the quenelles in a frying pan. Carefully unwrap the plastic wrap from the quenelles and roll them in the hot pan to brown slightly. Lift the quenelles onto kitchen paper to drain, then place them on warmed plates and spoon over the sauce.

POINTS TO WATCH

Keep everything cold. The fish will tighten up when chilled, holding the other ingredients together much better.

Poach the quenelles in hot but not boiling water. They are fragile at every stage. If the water is too hot they will start to soufflé, but you can put things right by adding some cold water.

The quenelles are cooked when the texture feels light and springs back when you prod them. Underdone quenelles will feel like wet cotton wool.

CRAB AND WINTER VEGETABLE SALAD WITH LEMON, HERB AND MUSTARD DRESSING

Dressed crab is a time-consuming dish, whether you stuff the crabmeat back into its shell in the traditional manner or, as here, use the cooked meat separately. The care with which the meat is picked from the claws and cartilage determines whether the dish is a pleasure or an adventure, for nothing spoils the appetite more quickly than a mouth full of sharp shell.

Sadly, frozen crabmeat is a mediocre product and will not substitute for fresh. Similarly, the crab dressed with stale chopped-up boiled egg and parsley that your fishmonger may sell is unlikely to be adequate either. They are typically cooked on the quayside by people taking no chances on the health front and with only limited interest on the gastronomic front. Dryness through overcooking is standard.

FOR 4 PERSONS

a few carrots

1 swede (rutabaga)

a few potatoes

1kg (2lb 4oz) crab

*2 tablespoons mayonnaise
    (page 47)*

1 tablespoon lemon juice

*1 teaspoon chopped
    parsley, or parsley
    dressing (page 49)*

1 teaspoon Dijon mustard

*1 teaspoon creamed
    horseradish*

*1 tablespoon vinaigrette
    (page 46)*

1 tablespoon olive oil

*a dash of Tabasco sauce,
    or more to taste*

salt and black pepper

Peel the root vegetables and cut them into 1cm (1/2in) dice. Boil until tender, then drain and set aside to cool.

In a large saucepan of simmering highly salted water, cook the crab for 30 minutes per kilo. Drain and let cool.

To dismantle the crab, break off the claws and legs. Crack them with one sharp tap using the back of a knife or a mallet – your aim is a clean break with the least splinters. Spoon the white meat into a container. Crack each of the thin legs and winkle out the meat with a needle.

Break off the tailflap on the centre of the main shell and pull out the body. Pull off and discard the rows of 'dead man's fingers' (the lungs) along each side.

Scoop out the brown meat from the rest of the shell, then pick out any meat you can find between the many layers and crevices of the main body, keeping the white and brown meats separate.

To dress the crab, carefully check the meat for any slivers of shell. Measure out an equal volume of vegetables to crabmeat.

Mix the mayonnaise, lemon juice and parsley with the white crabmeat and taste to check the seasoning. Mix the mustard, horseradish and vinaigrette with the brown meat. Toss the root vegetables in the olive oil, Tabasco and some salt and pepper.

If you want the dish to look like a restaurant offering, use a round pastry cutter as a mould for each plate, then spoon in the diced vegetables, the brown meat and finally the white meat in layers. Alternatively, spoon the layers into ramekins and serve.

POINTS TO WATCH

If you are going to boil the crab yourself, which is best, you must put plenty of salt in the cooking water, but don't use it as stock afterwards.

Try not to cook the beasts too long. All they need is 30 minutes per 1kg (2lb 4oz) in a large pan of simmering water.

When you are picking out the meat, you are unlikely to see all the tiny fragments of shell, but you will be able to feel them between your fingers and thumb if you concentrate your mind. Wash your hands thoroughly first and use latex gloves if you have them. But sort through the lot.

SCALLOP SALAD WITH SESAME DRESSING

This dish works on the same principle and basic method as the grilled cod with bitter salad leaves and parsley dressing (page 49) but has a very different, Oriental flavour. I'm not a fan of the corals, but this recipe will work just as well if you want to cook them along with the white scallop meat.

FOR 4 PERSONS

a selection of salad leaves
12 extra-fine french (green)
  beans, cooked
1 teaspoon light sesame oil
12 scallops
1 teaspoon sunflower oil
1 tablespoon sesame seeds
1/2 lemon

FOR THE DRESSING
50ml (2floz/1/4 cup) fish
  stock or water
50ml (2floz/1/4 cup) light
  sesame oil
25ml (1floz/2 tablespoons)
  sunflower oil
1 tablespoon coriander
  (cilantro) leaves
1 tablespoon pine nuts
1 tablespoon lemon juice
1 teaspoon chopped fresh
  ginger
1 teaspoon chopped shallot
1 teaspoon dark soy sauce
a dash of Tabasco sauce

Blend all the ingredients for the dressing in a blender and set aside until ready to serve.

Toss the salad leaves and beans in a few drops of sesame oil and place at the centre of each serving plate.

Heat a dry frying pan until it almost smokes. Slice the scallops into thickish coins and brush very lightly with sunflower oil.

Working in one-portion batches, place the scallops carefully onto the hot pan. Turn them over almost immediately – they should be golden brown but barely cooked in the middle.

Lift out onto paper towels and squeeze a few drops of lemon juice on top. Sprinkle with sesame seeds. Repeat the process until all the scallops are cooked.

Spoon the thick sesame dressing around the plates and lay the cooked scallops on top.

POINTS TO WATCH
Choose diver-caught scallops rather than those that have been dredged. The former cost more but have no nasty smells, sand or grit to contend with.

BRAISED COCKLES AND MUSSELS WITH PARSLEY FRIED BREAD

The wonderful flavour of cockles belie their low price. They are worth buying merely for the quality of stock they produce, however they can also be used instead of clams in any pasta dish. The Welsh coast provides tons of these molluscs but most go straight to the pickling plants.

FOR 4 PERSONS

500g (1lb 2oz/2 cups)
cockles or littleneck clams
500g (1lb 2oz/2 cups)
mussels
100ml (3 1/2floz/1/2 cup)
white wine
2 shallots, chopped
2 cloves garlic, chopped
2 tomatoes, skinned,
deseeded and diced
2 tablespoons tomato
passata (sieved tomatoes)
1/2 small fresh chilli
salt and pepper
FOR THE FRIED BREAD
4 tablespoons olive oil
4 slices white bread
4 tablespoons chopped
parsley

To make the fried bread, heat the olive oil in a frying pan and fry the bread on each side until golden. Place half the chopped parsley on a plate and dip the slices of fried bread in it to coat. Set aside in a warm place until ready to serve.

Place the cleaned cockles and mussels in a large pan and pour in the wine. Cover with a lid and bring to the boil for about 2 minutes. When the shells open, they are cooked.

Strain off the liquor and reserve. Pick half the cockles and mussels from their shells and leave the rest.

Fry the shallots and garlic in olive oil until golden. Add the diced tomato, passata and then the chilli. Cook for a few minutes, then add the cooking liquor.

Bring to the boil and simmer for a further 2 minutes before adding the shellfish to the sauce. Season with salt and pepper, then stir in the remaining chopped parsley. Serve with the bread.

POINTS TO WATCH

Cockles and mussels can be gritty. Wash them in several changes of cold water, or leave them in a bucket of water for an hour before cooking.

The shells are attractive and do not interfere unduly with the eating process. If half the shellfish are picked from the shells and half left in peace the result will look good and taste good.

The advantage of starting a restaurant where there was none before lies in the clean slate you start with. The house we chose had been much loved and looked after, not bashed about by disgruntled persons in white chefs' outfits. There were no unloved catering-standard tables and chairs that we would prefer not to have but could not justify replacing, no crew of any description left over from a previous arrangement to tells us that all our plans had been tried before and found not to work. Best of all, there were no existing customers to turn up and ask for the previous repertoire of dishes, or to tell all their friends how we had spoilt their favourite restaurant.

On the debit side, there was a dinky domestic kitchen with carpet on the floor, designed only to cope with the occasional dinner party and in need of a full set of protective armour for the hammering it was about to take. We bought the least and the cheapest equipment we could. Good cooking is about taste, care and skill I told myself, not fancy equipment. But I wasn't entirely sure.

The composition of the menu is important in that it either attracts or repels diners and its wording reflects the style of the cooking. Prices dictate the level of expectation in all sorts of areas, not just food, but also service and comfort. The style of food and number of dishes dictate the kitchen workload and their cost determine whether or not there is some chance of making a profit. How these conflicting pressures are juggled would decide whether or not we were in business for long. That and how well we cook the grub of course.

BRESAOLA

Bresaola and bündnerfleisch are cured and dried beef, from Italy and Switzerland respectively. Like Parma ham, they need to be sliced paper-thin and this can prove more difficult than any other part of the preparation. A kind word to your local butcher or delicatessen at slicing time is the answer.

This recipe comes from Franco Taruschio at the Walnut Tree Inn in Wales and I have used it for years. For a while saltpetre was awkward to obtain because it was an ingredient in explosives as well as ham brines, but you should be able to purchase it from chemists.

FOR 12 PERSONS

2kg (4lb 8oz) beef topside
FOR THE BRINE
1/2 bottle red wine
450g (1lb/1 2/3 cups) salt
200g (7oz/1 1/2 cups)
*   carrots, sliced*
100g (3 1/2oz/1/2 cup
*   packed) brown sugar*
6 chillies
1 tablespoon black
*   peppercorns*
1 tablespoon crushed
*   juniper berries*
1 teaspoon saltpetre
1 cinnamon stick
1 sprig thyme
TO SERVE
shaved Parmigiano
*   Reggiano cheese*
olive oil
black pepper

Combine all the ingredients for the brine in a large saucepan with 600ml (1 pint 2floz/2 3/4 cups) of water. Bring to the boil, then set aside to cool.

Put the meat in a bucket or a deep tray and pour on the brine. Leave this to marinate for 4 days in a cool place or in the fridge.

Lift the meat from the brine and pat dry with paper towels. Wrap it in cheesecloth and hang in a dry, warm place for two weeks or until the meat is quite firm when pressed.

The meat won't look pretty at this point, like something from King Tut's tomb, but cut away the dried outside layer and you will be left with a deep purple block. This is the bresaola.

Slice the meat thinly – a shop slicing machine is ideal – then dress with shavings of Parmesan, black pepper and olive oil.

VARIATIONS
Instead of the Parmigiano Reggiano, some cooked vegetable salad in vinaigrette will also fit the bill and contrast nicely with the texture of the meat.

POINTS TO WATCH
If the meat isn't completely covered by the brine, don't worry. Simply turn it each day and extend the marinating period by two days.

Air has to circulate around the beef as it dries so try not to have one side resting against a wall or work surface.

GARLIC AND CHICKEN LIVER TART WITH SALADS IN WALNUT DRESSING

Quiches suffer from past over-popularity, also from the penny-pinching of companies mass-producing them for the supermarket trade. Well-made versions with proper eggs, cream and some flavouring other than cheese and ham, are an eye-opener to the delicious possibilities.

FOR 6 PERSONS

FOR THE PASTRY

*1 medium (large) egg, plus
    a little beaten egg for
    brushing*
*160g (5 1/2oz/1 1/4 stick)
    unsalted butter, softened*
*250g (9oz) plain flour
    (2 cups unbleached
    all-purpose flour)*
1 teaspoon salt
1 tablespoon milk

FOR THE FILLING

*150g (5oz/scant 1/2 cup)
    chicken livers, trimmed*
1 shallot, chopped
2 cloves garlic, chopped
3 medium (large) eggs
*250ml (9floz/1 cup)
    double (heavy) cream*
1 tablespoon brandy
1 tablespoon basil leaves
a little grated nutmeg
salt and pepper

FOR THE SALAD

a selection of salad leaves
1 avocado, sliced
*1 tablespoon toasted
    pine nuts*
1 tablespoon walnut oil
1 teaspoon sherry vinegar

To make the pastry, stir the egg and softened butter together, then rub the mixture into the flour and salt. When almost amalgamated, add the milk and knead two or three times so that everything is well mixed. Rest the pastry for at least 1 hour.

Heat the oven to 200°C (400°F/Gas 6). Roll out the pastry and use it to line a 26cm (10in) tart tin – preferably one with a detachable base. Brush the tart case with a little beaten egg, then bake for 10 minutes. Remove from the oven and lower the temperature to 150°C (300°F/Gas 2)

For the filling, purée the chicken livers, shallot and garlic in a blender or food processor. Add the eggs and cream, mix briefly, then add the brandy, basil, nutmeg and some salt and pepper and blend well. There should be a total of just under 1 litre (1 pint 15floz/4 1/2 cups) of mixture.

Pour the filling into the tart case and bake for about 30 minutes or until firm and set. Unmould the quiche and leave to settle for a few minutes before cutting into wedges.

Combine the salad leaves, avocado and pine nuts in a salad bowl, then dress with the walnut oil and sherry vinegar. Season to taste and serve the salad around the warm tart.

POINTS TO WATCH

It is dispiriting to see the filling leak out from tiny gaps in the pastry case. Brush the base and sides with a little beaten egg to seal any holes.

Some people like to line a pastry case with beans or some-such so that it doesn't bubble up while cooking. I am not a fan of this technique and find that the base doesn't cook properly under all that weight. A good rest in the fridge works wonders and, should the pastry rise in patches, it can be gently pressed back down with no damage done.

The tart needs to bake at a moderate temperature once the filling is added. An oven that is too hot will cause the filling to soufflé up and then sink, which means the texture of the finished dish will suffer.

ESHLY CUT

SPARAGUS

Vegetable cookery

MR S. HILL
THE MERCHANT HOUSE
LOWER CORVE ST.
LUDLOW
SHROPSHIRE   SY 8
               1DU

INTERLINK EXPRESS   01299
                     250697

12

2333211551

CONSIGN No: 0460346370/1

RESHLY CUT

ASPARAGUS

In a commercial kitchen, the vegetable chef's position is usually the most junior and least well paid in the scheme of things and this reflects the low esteem in which vegetable cookery is held. Vegetables served as side dishes ought to contribute some quality of taste or texture, not just occupy space on the plate. This holds true whether they are served alongside everything else or exiled to serving bowls in the middle of the table.

Try not to choose side vegetables purely to suit a colour scheme. Half the carrots served may well have been chosen only to form part of an attractive duo alongside peas, sprouts or broccoli. Carrots are sweet, sprouts have a pronounced cabbage smell; both can be a delight and work wonderfully with late season lamb or partridge, but not with everything.

The majority of side vegetables are simply boiled so as not to upstage the star item on the plate. Good restaurants usually dress the hot vegetables by tossing them in a butter emulsion (a little water is boiled and seasoned, then pieces of unsalted butter are whisked in) and

Try not to choose side vegetables purely to suit a colour scheme.

this will lightly coat the vegetables, evenly distributing the seasoning but not leaving them greasy. A tiny quantity of good oil and a few drops of the cooking water will do the same job.

Perversely, the vegetables in a vegetarian meal can be as peripheral as in a meat or fish meal. Best are the dishes that have no meat-substitute overtones and are satisfying in their own right. Most cereals such as rice or couscous go well with grilled or braised vegetables or a mixture of tomato and herbs. If the results look a little shapeless, somehow less imposing or significant, then you have a presentation problem rather than one of content – time to dig out more attractive serving dishes and prepare some fresh herb garnishes.

Just as in a meat-based meal, making the most of cheap ingredients involves a greater commitment of time and imagination. A dish of steamed asparagus with melted butter or even hollandaise sauce is a far easier option than a tempura or stuffed aubergine in the same way as a grilled chop presents less work than a well-made stew.

For much of the world's population, meat and fish play a minor role in the daily diet anyway, and not just for philosopical or religious reasons, so it's always worth exploring the cuisines of the Eastern Mediterranean and Middle East as well as Buddhist and other cultures for inspiration. The transformation of simple chickpeas (garbanzos) and broad beans (fava) into treats such as hummus and falafel, or even sugar syrup and cornstarch into Turkish delight, gives plenty of scope to anyone feeling a touch jaded.

SWEDE AND CHEDDAR SOUFFLÉ

Soufflés rarely taste of much, the large volume of whisked egg white deadens most flavours. Those that work best rely on powerful ingredients such as chocolate or passionfruit. Savoury soufflés are usually cheese-based, often Gruyère, and can have the same problem. Extra cheese improves the flavour but gives a gooey mixture that is inclined to slide down the side of the soufflé dish as it cooks rather than towering erect above it. This swede (rutabaga) and Cheddar version succeeds on the flavour front but will need a collar to create the full visual effect.

FOR 4 PERSONS

450g (1lb) swede (rutabaga), peeled and diced
50g (2oz/1/2 stick) unsalted butter
40g (1 1/2oz/4 tablespoons) plain (all-purpose) flour
a little milk (optional)
6 large eggs, separated
1/4 teaspoon cream of tartar
175g (6oz/1 1/2 cups) grated Cheddar cheese
salt and black pepper

Boil the swede in a covered pan until tender – this will take around 25 minutes depending on the size of your dice. When cooked, drain the water into a jug for later use.

Wipe the pan clean then, over a low heat, melt the butter. Stir in the flour to make a roux, then cook gently for 1 minute.

Measure out 350ml (12floz/1 1/2 cups) of the swede cooking water, making up the difference with some milk if necessary. Pour this liquid, one-third at a time, onto the roux, stirring after each addition, until the sauce reboils and thickens.

Heat the oven to 200°C (400°F/Gas 6). Mash the swede and season it with salt and pepper. Stir in the sauce, then the egg yolks. Make sure everything is well mixed.

In a large bowl, whisk the egg whites with the cream of tartar and 1/4 teaspoon of salt until stiff.

Turn the swede mixture into a bowl and stir in one-quarter of the whisked egg white. This will loosen it enough to successfully fold in the remaining egg white and the grated Cheddar.

Spoon the mixture into a buttered 1 litre (13/4 pint/4 1/2 cup) soufflé dish – collar attached – trying not to spill too much around the rim of the dish or onto its collar.

Bake the soufflé for 45 minutes. Remove the collar and serve as soon as possible.

POINTS TO WATCH

You must preheat the oven.

The sides of the soufflé dish need to be well buttered, especially at the rim. If the mixture sticks on one side of the rim, the soufflé will form a bellows shape, rising on one side only. If both sides stick, it will not rise at all.

The soufflé dish needs a collar. Oil or butter a double-folded strip of greaseproof paper, baking parchment or foil wide enough and long enough to fit around the dish and rise 5cm (2in) above it. An elastic band will keep it in place.

Soufflés are not as fragile as you might imagine. Don't be afraid to open the oven door and check the progress.

The swede can be prepared in advance. This recipe calls for the water in which they were boiled to be added but milk can be used instead.

SICILIAN BAKED COURGETTE WITH ORANGE, PINE NUTS AND HERBS

Stuffed vegetables have a long history. The Eastern Mediterranean has stuffed vine leaves and aubergine (eggplant) while Middle Europe stuffs cabbage and bell peppers. Usually it makes sense to push the stuffing back into the vegetable shell but it's not compulsory and, if you prefer, some pastry (filo or puff in the case of this stuffing mixture) will do the job just as well.

FOR 4 PERSONS

4 large courgettes (zucchini)

FOR THE STUFFING

1 medium red onion, finely chopped

120ml (4floz/1/2 cup) olive oil

90g (31/2oz/13/4 cups) fresh white breadcrumbs

12 pitted green olives, roughly chopped

2 tablespoons pine nuts

2 tablespoons currants

2 tablespoons chopped parsley

1 tablespoon small capers

the juice of 1 orange

salt and pepper

To make the stuffing, fry the onion in a little of the olive oil until it starts to colour. Stir in the breadcrumbs and continue cooking for another 2 to 3 minutes.

Stir in the remaining stuffing ingredients and season the mixture with salt and pepper. Leave to cool.

Peel away alternate strips of skin from the courgettes. Cook the courgettes in boiling water for 2 minutes, then drain them and cool under cold running water.

Halve the courgettes lengthways. Brush them with olive oil and sprinkle a little salt and pepper over them. Press the stuffing onto the cut halves.

Brush over any remaining olive oil then bake the courgettes in a preheated oven at 200°C (400°F/Gas 6) for 20 minutes. Alternatively, grill or broil them gently until crisp.

POINTS TO WATCH

Make sure the courgettes are fully cooked before you stuff and grill or broil them. They will not change texture during this last stage of cooking.

WARM CELERIAC MOUSSE WITH MUSHROOM SAUCE

Celeriac and mushrooms are particularly compatible. Having some wild mushrooms dotted about the plate too makes this dish even better. The combination of mushrooms and celeriac will also compliment dark game dishes of venison or hare.

FOR 4 PERSONS

FOR THE MOUSSE

*1 medium celeriac
   (celery root), about
   600g (1lb 5oz)*

*150ml (5floz/10 table-
   spoons) double (heavy)
   cream*

2 eggs

*1 teaspoon creamed
   horseradish*

salt and pepper

FOR THE SAUCE

*250g (9oz) button
   mushrooms*

*50g (2oz/1/2 cup) shallots,
   chopped*

*100ml (3 1/2floz/1/2 cup)
   olive oil*

*100ml (3 1/2floz/1/2 cup)
   white wine or stock*

Peel and dice the celeriac. Boil it in a covered saucepan of water until tender, then drain.

Purée the cooked celeriac in a blender with the cream, eggs, horseradish and some salt and pepper.

Heat the oven to 150°C (300°F/Gas 2). Line four ramekin dishes with food-friendly plastic wrap, then fill with the celeriac mixture. Place in a roasting tray and half-fill the tray with lukewarm water. Bake until set – this should take around 25 minutes.

To make the sauce, chop the mushrooms finely. Cook them with the shallots in a small saucepan with a few drops of the olive oil and some salt and pepper. Add the wine or stock.

Purée the mushroom mixture, along with the remaining olive oil, in the blender. Pour the sauce onto warmed serving plates, then turn out the mousses, laying them on top of the pools of mushroom sauce.

POINTS TO WATCH

A food processor will finely chop the mushrooms in seconds, provided you cut them into quarters first, and think that cleaning the equipment after-wards is an easier task than chopping mushrooms by hand.

VEGETABLE TEMPURA

Successful tempura has two essentials, well-made batter and well-judged deep-frying. Most restaurants buy tempura batter from Oriental supermarkets as a ready-made mix, just as most fish and chip shops buy in the batter that coats their offerings.

It's customary to deep-fry some slivers of fish or shellfish in addition to the vegetables but the dish works just as well without, or even as part of a salad with the dipping sauce doubling as dressing for the greens. Dashi is bonito tuna stock, available dried in sachets in Oriental shops and delicatessens.

FOR 4 PERSONS

FOR THE BATTER

250ml (9floz/1 cup +
   2 tablespoons) very cold
   iced water
1 medium egg
100g (4oz/1 cup) plain
   (all-purpose) flour
50g (2oz/1/2 cup) cornflour
   (cornstarch)
a pinch of salt
vegetable oil, for frying

FOR THE VEGETABLES

2 red bell peppers
1 aubergine (eggplant)
2 courgettes (zucchini)
4 spring onions (scallions)
8 shiitake, girolle or button
   mushrooms

FOR THE DIPPING SAUCE

4 tablespoons dashi
2 tablespoons Japanese
   soy sauce
1 teaspoon finely chopped
   fresh ginger
1 small chilli, finely chopped
1/2 teaspoon sugar

First prepare the vegetables. Halve and deseed the bell peppers, then cut them into 10cm (4in) strips. Peel the aubergine and cut into 10cm (4in) batons. Cut the courgette into 10cm (4in) batons. Wash, top and tail the spring onions and wash and slice the mushrooms.

Make the dipping sauce by combining all the ingredients in a small bowl.

Make the batter by stirring together the cold water, egg, plain flour, cornflour and salt in a large bowl.

Heat the oil – to 190°C (375°F) if you have a thermometer – then dip the vegetable slices in the batter and deep-fry. Drain on kitchen paper and serve with the dipping sauce.

POINTS TO WATCH

Temperatures are important. The batter must be cold and the frying oil hot if the tempura is to be light and crisp.

Handle the batter as little as possible even if this means leaving a few lumps.

If making the batter ahead of the cooking time, keep it in a bowl surrounded by ice cubes.

Don't try to cook vast batches of the tempura at one time. This lowers the temperature of the oil substantially and may result in one large greasy fritter rather than delicate morsels.

A wok will use less oil than a conventional deep-fryer.

The vegetables are cooked from raw, not parboiled. Therefore the thickness of the slices needs thought; too thick and they will take forever to cook; too thin and you will taste only the batter.

Preparing globe artichokes

You need a bowl or bin over which to trim the artichokes, a small container of lemon juice, and a pot or saucepan pan large enough to cook the vegetables. This should contain some cold water, salt, and a little white wine. You will also need a circle of greaseproof or parchment paper, cut to fit neatly across the top of the pot, and two knives, one serrated (a bread knife is fine) and a small sharp one, like a chef's turning knife, for trimming.

Use the serrated knife to cut a thin slice from the base and sides of the globe, then cut off the top section of the artichoke at the point about 4cm (1 1/2in) up from its base. Use the small knife to trim away the remaining leaves and any bristly or green patches – they will turn brown once cooked. Drop the artichoke into the lemon juice, then put it in the pan of water. Repeat with each artichoke. The circle of paper is used to cover the artichokes while simmering and the hairy chokes are removed from the hearts after cooking.

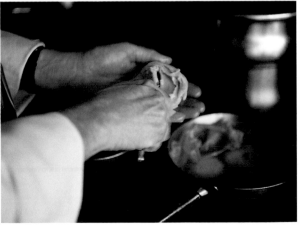

WARM ARTICHOKE HEART WITH PEAS AND MINT HOLLANDAISE SAUCE

Globe artichokes are daunting. They produce a disproportionate ratio of debris to edible parts and the hairy choke can seem impossible to loosen. Classical cuisine calls for them to be cooked in a blanc, a mixture of flour, lemon juice and water. This succeeds in keeping the hearts white but leaves a slimy coating – often an uncleanable saucepan as well.

Organizing a small production line as on the previous pages will make the process simple. If this seems an absurd performance for a few vegetables, the results should compensate. Once this setup is in place you can as easily prepare six or 60 artichokes. Perhaps the moral here is to cook artichokes for large parties and not impromptu lunches.

FOR 4 PERSONS

4 large globe artichokes

3 tablespoons lemon juice

4 tablespoons white wine

1 batch of hollandaise sauce (page 32)

1 tablespoon chopped fresh mint

100g (3 1/2oz/3/4 cup) shelled peas

Prepare the artichokes as described on the previous page.

Cover the pan with a circle of greaseproof (parchment) paper and boil the artichokes gently until they are tender enough to pierce easily with the tip of a sharp knife, about 20 minutes. Remove from the heat and allow to cool in the cooking liquor.

Make the hollandaise sauce as directed on page 32, then add the chopped fresh mint.

To complete the dish, lift the artichokes from the cooking liquid and spoon away the hairy fibres from the centre of each one. Reheat the hearts in some of the cooking liquor.

Boil and roughly mash the peas. Spoon some in the centre of each artichoke heart, place on a serving plate and spoon over the hollandaise sauce. Serve immediately.

POINTS TO WATCH

If you have sensitive skin, it would be wise to wear kitchen gloves while trimming the artichokes. They are, after all, a type of thistle.

This method assumes you are preparing the artichokes ahead of time, which is easier and more sensible. If you plan to serve the artichokes as soon as they are cooked, you will need to scrape out the furry choke section while the vegetables are still hot. Once again you will need kitchen gloves.

RAGOÛT OF WILD MUSHROOMS AND SUMMER VEGETABLES

Wild mushrooms are available year round, but they are not always good value or good to eat. The season in Britain begins mid-summer with girolles and progresses to the boletus family (porcini or ceps) soon after. Morels come in spring and the others (cauliflower fungus, beefsteak and the like), you will find on mid-summer walks in the woods. There is no formal set of ingredients to this dish; those here are only a guideline based on the market one fine summer day at the tail-end of the asparagus season.

FOR 4 PERSONS

8 baby artichokes
the juice of 1 lemon
a bunch of small carrots
250g (9oz/1 3/4 cups) broad
   (fava) beans
4 small leeks
8 asparagus spears
200g (7oz/1 cup) sugar
   snap peas
200g (7oz/2 1/2 cups) mixed
   girolle and black trumpet
   mushrooms
1 tablespoon grated
   Parmesan cheese
1 tablespoon olive oil, plus
   extra oil or butter for frying
1 teaspoon crème fraîche
salt

Cut the outer leaves from the artichokes, then cut each globe in four lengthways. Boil them in a pan of lemon juice and salted water until tender, about 10 minutes.

Peel and scrape the vegetables as necessary. Remove the inner skins from the broad beans as well as the pods.

Bring 250ml (9floz/1 cup) of water to the boil, then add the vegetables in the order they need to be cooked: carrots first and sugar snaps last. The whole process shouldn't take more than 6 or 7 minutes. Then add the cooked artichokes.

Fry the mushrooms in a little olive oil and set aside. Lift the vegetables from the cooking liquid and scatter them on warmed serving bowls. Top with the cooked mushrooms.

Add the pan juices from the wild mushrooms to the water in which the vegetables were cooked. Put this in a blender with the Parmesan, olive oil and crème fraîche and process to a smooth, light sauce. Check the sauce for seasoning, then pour it over the vegetables and serve.

POINTS TO WATCH

The wild mushrooms will produce a lot of cooking liquid that eliminates the need for stock when added to the sauce. Let all their liquid drain back into the pan and before adding it to the cooking liquid of the other vegetables.

A restaurant kitchen runs differently from a domestic one. The dishes in a restaurant are broken down like Lego into components, some of which are applicable to more than one dish. Things like chopped shallots, chicken stock and diced tomato, for instance, can be prepared in quantity and in advance.

Mornings and afternoons are spent skimming stockpots and preparing this sort of thing, the results of which are known as the mise-en-place. If you see the chef turn up at the same time as the diners, there are only two serious possibilities: elves and fairies make it all, or the chef buys in the dishes ready prepared.

The restaurant service, the time when lunch or dinner is actually being served and eaten, is a matter of cooking the trimmed pieces of meat and fish and assembling the ingredients of each dish from the little containers of chopped herbs and pots of reduced stock. This is why restaurant dishes can be awkward to reproduce at home, where the fridge may not contain carefully prepared fresh breadcrumbs or mushroom stuffing. The consolation is that straightforward dishes like roast Aylesbury duck are difficult to serve in good restaurants because the duck takes longer to cook than customers are prepared to wait and will be mediocre if precooked then heated up.

Strangely, everything is on both a larger and smaller scale than at home. Big pots of fish stock are made but single portions of a dish are put together and cooked at the time of each order. Visitors to the kitchen are always surprised by the quantity of tiny saucepans and frying pans found there, forgetting that they have just participated in a meal where everybody ate something different.

CARROT AND SPRING ONION FRITTERS

Side dishes of vegetables can be lifted with a change of cooking method. Standard boiling and steaming will never give a crisp texture and there are occasions when this may enhance a dish. Serve these fritters with the mackerel on page 98, or with steamed or poached dishes of fish and chicken.

FOR 4 - 8 FRITTERS

50g (2oz/1/2 cup)
carrot, coarsely grated
40g (11/2oz/1/3 cup) spring
onions (scallions), sliced
2 tablespoons fresh white
breadcrumbs
1 large egg, beaten
vegetable oil, for frying

Mix the carrot, spring onion and breadcrumbs in a bowl, then stir in the beaten egg.

Heat the oil to a depth of 2.5cm (1in) in a frying pan. Drop the carrot mixture into the oil a tablespoonful at a time. Cook on each side until crisp, about 2 or 3 minutes.

POINTS TO WATCH
Don't start frying the fritters until the oil is hot and, to maintain the temperature, cook them in two batches rather than overcrowd the pan.

TIAN OF AUBERGINE

Tian is part of that collection of words, like timbale or cocotte, which give a dish the name of the pot in which it is cooked or served rather than an ingredient or cooking process. A tian is an earthenware dish from Provence with a wide rim tapering quickly down to a narrow base, thus giving a good ratio of crisp topping to rather less soft filling. By association, a tian is any dish cooked this way. This could be served as a first course or light lunch with salad, or as a partner to roast lamb or veal.

FOR 4 PERSONS

1 tablespoon lemon juice
1 kg (2lb 4oz) aubergines
(eggplant)
450g (1lb) plum tomatoes,
skinned, deseeded and
cut into small dice
a bunch of basil, finely
chopped
225g (8oz/2 cups) grated
Gruyère cheese
a little butter or oil, for
greasing

Heat the oven to 180°C (350°F/Gas 4). Bring a pan of salted water to the boil and add the lemon juice.

Slice the aubergine into rounds and drop them into the boiling water. Cook for 1 minute, then drain well.

Layer the aubergine slices alternately with the diced tomato in a greased ovenproof dish. Top with the basil and Gruyère, then bake for 40 minutes, until golden on top.

POINTS TO WATCH
In any layered vegetable dish it is important to have layers of the same size, or that they get smaller as they go up, because otherwise the ingredients could collapse when cooked. Putting the ballast at the bottom is a basic building technique.

BAKED BEANS

This is a slow recipe, not a spur of the moment item like its famous counterpart in the turquoise can. Boston baked beans, of which this is a version, are quite sweet and the two main flavours other than sugar are mustard and tomato. Any other addition is a matter of personal preference. During a stint in the kitchen of a Hungarian restaurant I developed a liking for their baked beans which included a fair amount of paprika, smoked pork and goose fat. Serve these with fatty, rich meats like duck.

FOR 4 PERSONS

*500g (1lb 2oz/3 cups) dried
    haricot or navy beans*
1 medium onion, chopped
2 cloves garlic, crushed
1 tablespoon vegetable oil
1 teaspoon paprika
*4 tablespoons tomato
    passata (sieved tomatoes)*
1 tablespoon mustard
*150g (5oz) fatty bacon,
    in one piece*
*75g (3oz/1/2 cup lightly
    packed) soft brown sugar*
2 tablespoons molasses
*a dash of Worcestershire
    sauce*
salt

Soak the beans overnight in double their volume of water. Next day, bring the beans to the boil and simmer for 10 minutes Drain, then rinse in cold water.

Heat the oven to 150°C (300°F/Gas 2). In a small pan, fry the onion and garlic in the oil, then stir in the paprika, followed by the tomato passata and mustard.

Put the piece of bacon in a heavy casserole and add the drained beans, onion mixture, then the sugar and molasses.

Pour in enough water to keep the beans moist – about 250ml (9floz/1 cup) should do – then cover and bake for 5 hours. Each hour, stir the beans and top up the water.

Finally, at the end of cooking, add salt to taste and a good dash of Worcestershire sauce.

POINTS TO WATCH

Do not add salt to the water during soaking or cooking. As with all pulse dishes, salt has to be added at the end of the proceedings or it will toughen the beans.

The beans are baked in a covered pot for 5 hours. In order that they do bake at this stage rather than stew or boil, the water level inside the pot is important. The surface of the liquid should be level with the beans but no more than that. The pot can be topped up a touch every hour so that the beans stay moist.

All beans have a reputation for causing wind. This can be alleviated by using fresh water to cook the beans rather than reusing the soaking liquid.

The starch component

The Ancient Greeks divided their meals into two components, filler and everything else. *Opson* was the word for the expensive, highly flavoured element and could be some treatment of fish or meat, or maybe just a sauce of cheese and herbs. *Sitos* was the starch element that formed the bulk of the meal and a backdrop to the *opson's* flavours. In those days the *sitos* would have been fine wheaten bread if you were well off, or barley porridge if you weren't.

The strength of the sauce or the seasoning of the fish or meat would be related to the amount of starch that needed flavouring, in the same way as, today, a tomato topping for pizza will be more highly flavoured than a tomato soup with croûtons. There was also an etiquette in operation and those who ate more than their fair share of sauce or *opson* in ancient times were considered rather gross.

Until fairly recently, the starch element of meals varied substantially from country to country. Climate and soil conditions dictated what was available and discoveries like the potato made a massive impact on national diets. With improved transportation and technology, there is now plenty of choice. Italy's pasta, America's cornmeal and Asia's rice are as easily obtained in Britain as spuds, but in most restaurants, potatoes are still more popular than the others. Indeed, it was not so long ago that people would expect to be served potatoes as a vegetable in addition to pasta or rice, instead of as the alternative they are considered today. Spaghetti and lasagne are as familiar to children in Ludlow as Bologna, though they might have a little more difficulty in recognizing the sauces that accompany them. The starch component is also a key factor in many vegetarian meals and chefs often use ingredients like pastry, pasta, rice or potato to form the base on which a vegetarian meal is built.

While it is sensible to consider dishes such as polenta or Indian flatbreads in the context of a national or regional cuisine – they have evolved around particular patterns of spicing and habits of eating – there is no reason why they have to be used solely for ethnic meals or

Spaghetti and lasagne are as familiar to children in Ludlow as Bologna.

even in any 'authentic' manner. The function performed by the starch content in a meal, that of satisfying the stomach and providing a vehicle for whatever flavours are being used, is what counts. If this seems a relatively humble task, it is worth remembering that the range of possibilities for the cook has never been greater. Substitute some couscous, rice or spaetzli for the potatoes usually served round your piece of roast lamb and you will have kept the balance of the meal but changed its style completely.

POTATO AND OLIVE CAKES

All potato-based cakes are made in a similar way. Fishcakes, corned beef hash, bubble and squeak and suchlike are all variations on the same idea and once you're adept at one, you've mastered them all. Olives may seem more at home with noodles than spuds, but they combine well, as you will see.

FOR 4 PERSONS

500g (1lb 2oz) potatoes
30 pitted green olives,
*   chopped*
1 tablespoon olive oil
1 egg, beaten, plus 1 yolk
1 tablespoon chopped
*   parsley*
100g (3 1/2oz/1 3/4 cups)
*   fresh breadcrumbs*
vegetable oil, for frying
salt and black pepper

Peel the potatoes and cut into pieces of approximately equal size. Boil them in salted water until tender. Drain and leave in the colander for a few moments to dry.

Push the potatoes through a sieve, then add the olives, olive oil, egg yolk, parsley and some salt and pepper. Stir together gently.

Compress the mixture into golfball-sized balls, then flatten them slightly into hamburger shapes. Dip the patties into the beaten egg, then coat with the fresh breadcrumbs. Fry in a warm oiled pan until browned on both sides and serve hot.

POINTS TO WATCH

Chose a variety of potato that is not too floury, for example Red Desirée or Yukon Gold.

Try to avoid a hard rolling boil while the potatoes are cooking. This will make the outer layer disintegrate before the centre is cooked and will result in watery potato cakes.

Handle the mashed potato as little as possible once it has been mashed or sieved. Also, the olives should be mixed in with the minimum of beating.

Crumbs from very fresh bread are difficult to use. Once dampened by contact with beaten egg they become stodgy and solid. Day-old bread is best. If your bread is too fresh, cut it into cubes and dry it out in a low oven for a short while.

Breadcrumbs can be made in a food processor by first removing the crusts and then cutting the inside into cubes before processing. The paddle attachment on a mixer will do the same job though not as quickly.

GRATIN POTATOES

There are two ways of making good gratin dauphinois. The traditional method calls for thinly sliced raw potatoes to be layered with Gruyère cheese and then topped with a 50:50 mixture of milk and cream. This needs an hour or longer to cook and should be eaten straightaway. At The Merchant House I make a variation on this called gratin de Jabron. It uses potatoes preboiled in their skins and can be made in 30 minutes. It also tastes better, more of potato and less of cream.

FOR 4 PERSONS

1kg (2lb 4oz) potatoes
20g (3/4oz/1 1/2 tablespoons)
*   unsalted butter*
3 large cloves garlic, crushed
300ml (10 1/2floz/1 1/3 cups)
*   milk*
300ml (10 1/2floz/1 1/3 cups)
*   double (heavy) cream*
50g (2oz/1/2 cup) grated
*   hard cheese, preferably*
*   Gruyère, Parmesan or*
*   mature Cheddar*
salt and black pepper

Wash the potatoes and boil them in their skins until cooked through. Drain, peel and cut into dice or slices as you fancy.

Working in batches if your frying pan is too small to fit all the potatoes, warm the butter with the crushed garlic. Season with plenty of salt and pepper, then add the potatoes and toss them – the object is to coat them with warm garlic butter, not to fry them. After this stage they can be kept for up to 24 hours ready to make the gratin when needed.

Heat the oven to 200°C (400°F/Gas 6). Spread the potatoes out in an ovenproof dish around 2.5cm (1in) deep. Pour on the milk and cream, top with grated cheese and bake for 30 minutes.

POINTS TO WATCH

The potatoes are boiled in their skins so need to be of roughly equal size if they are to cook evenly. Sort through them before weighing.

Unless you have a really large wok or frying pan, you will need to work in two or three batches to toss all the potato in the garlic-flavoured butter.

POTATO GNOCCHI

Gnocchi are dumplings. They come in many styles and can be made from plain flour, semolina or, as here, potato. This mixture is similar to that used in Ulster, Northern Ireland, to make potato bread, the idea being to incorporate plenty of flour into a base of mashed potato, then bind the two with egg. Whereas good Ulster folk griddle the result to accompany bacon rashers and fried egg, Italians cut the mixture into little dumplings for poaching.

FOR 4-6 PERSONS

1kg (2lb 4oz) potatoes,
* peeled*
2 eggs
30g (1oz/1/4 cup) grated
* Parmesan cheese*
a little grated nutmeg
350g (12oz/2 1/3 cups)
* plain (all-purpose) flour*
salt and pepper

Boil the potatoes, then mash them. Place the mash in a large bowl then gently work in the eggs, Parmesan, nutmeg, some salt and pepper and all but a tablespoon of the flour (the rest will be needed to dust the gnocchi before they are poached).

Form the mixture into a ball then, with the palms of your hands, roll the dough into cylinders the thickness of good cigars. Cut the cylinders into 2cm (3/4in) pieces and dust with flour.

Bring a large pan of salted water to the boil. As you do so, press one side of the gnocchi against a fork or grater to make ridges, then drop them into the boiling water. They will rise to the surface as they cook. Lift them out with a slotted spoon.

The gnocchi are ready. Just before serving, toss them in a pan with butter or whatever sauce you fancy.

POINTS TO WATCH

Do not add any butter, olive oil or milk when mashing the potatoes and try not to overhandle them or they will become gluey.

Gnocchi should be slightly ridged – this is best done by pressing them against a fork or a box grater.

FRESH GOATS' CHEESE GNOCCHI

Semolina flour, from which this is made, is the name for a grade of milled wheat that can be made into a sweet or savoury porridge. Unlike polenta, the cornmeal porridge that needs to be boiled a good half hour, semolina cooks quickly and needs only be brought to the boil.

The idea here is that the cereal should be cooked with flavoursome ingredients such as cheese and eggs, allowed to set, then cut into shapes for grilling or broiling and baking. It can be served with a robust concoction of tomato and herbs, or with venison or partridge.

FOR 4 PERSONS

500ml (18floz/2 1/4 cups)
  milk
a little grated nutmeg
150g (5oz/3/4 cup)
  semolina
25g (1oz/1/4 cup) grated
  Parmesan cheese
1 egg
100g (3 1/2oz/scant 1/2 cup)
  fresh goats' cheese
oil, for greasing
salt and pepper

In a saucepan, season the milk with salt, pepper and nutmeg. Mix in the semolina and bring to the boil, stirring continuously. The mixture will thicken to the point where it is almost solid. Stir in the grated Parmesan and egg.

Pour half the semolina mixture into an oiled tray. Slice the fresh goats' cheese and lay it on top of the first layer before pouring on the remaining semolina mixture.

Heat the oven to 180°C (350°F/Gas 4). Cover the gnocchi with a piece of buttered greaseproof or parchment paper, or some greased plastic wrap, and place in a roasting tray half-filled with warm water. Bake for 25 minutes.

Remove the gnocchi from the oven and leave to cool. Cut it into squares – or whatever shape takes your fancy.

To gratinate, heat a frying pan and grease it with a few drops of olive oil. Add the gnocchi, stir to coat, then put the pan on the base of a hot oven for 10 minutes to give a dark golden brown crust underneath. The gnocchi are then lifted and turned upside down onto the plate to serve.

POINTS TO WATCH

The depth of the tray will equal the height of the gnocchi, so choose carefully, around 3cm (1 1/4 in) is ideal.

You can gratinate the gnocchi under a hot grill or broiler but I prefer the method given here.

The mealtime service in restaurants has theatrical overtones. The cook makes preparations as best he or she can and hopes that everyone will really enjoy the food – not from any good-natured desire to please, rather as a reassurance that the dishes which represent all our skill and taste really are okay. We hope those dining pitch up in a steady progression rather than a cavalry charge at eight o'clock so that a decent amount of time may be given to cooking each dish. Tension rises, but also a euphoria that may switch quite quickly to anger if things go badly. What a good psychiatrist would make of it all, I'm not sure.

The set up at The Merchant House has never allowed the luxury of kitchen tantrums. Neither Anja nor our waitress would stand for it and there is, in any case, no time. Part of my tiny and invaluable cooking space is used to house a radio and CD player so there is music in the kitchen. Mozart's operas play almost constantly, usually Don Giovanni with Figaro as second preference. This soothes when things turn difficult – those occasions when I have wrongly guessed the relative popularity of the day's dishes and am furiously filleting extra fish, or am remaking a sauce that has become too warm and split into an unsightly mess of oil and stock.

The music also acts as barrier between my own comments and the delicate ears of customers only two metres distant who are midway through a cosy dinner and might not want to hear my forthright views on their previously unannounced allergy to everything on the menu.

SPAETZLI

Spaetzli are dumplings made from wheat flour. They are commonly served with game stews in Alsace and Switzerland. A similar recipe is used in Hungary to produce almost identical dumplings called galuska which are the usual accompaniment to gulyas and paprika chicken.

The word spaetzli apparently translates as 'little sparrows' for reasons that escape me. They are made from a thick pancake batter which is pushed through a colander into boiling salted water, and the resulting strands of dough are then tossed in butter. Spaetzli may sound awful, but in fact tastes very good and provides an unobtrusive yet appealing foil to any well-flavoured stew.

FOR 4 PERSONS

300g (10 1/2oz) plain four
(2 heaping cups
all-purpose flour)
3 medium (large) eggs
75ml (3floz/ 1/3 cup) milk
2 teaspoons vegetable oil
a little grated nutmeg
50g (2oz/ 1/2 stick) butter
salt and pepper

Mix together the flour, eggs, milk, oil, a little grated nutmeg, 1 level teaspoon of salt and 100ml (3 1/2floz/7 tablespoons) of water to make a batter. Leave it to rest for 30 minutes.

Bring a large pan of salted water to the boil, then push the batter through a colander or spaetzli machine. Alternatively, cut the batter into ribbons and add it to the water.

As soon as the spaetzli float to the surface, they are ready. Scoop them out with a slotted spoon. If they are not to be used immediately, cool them in cold water, then drain, place in a bowl and cover with plastic wrap.

Just before serving, heat the butter in a frying pan and toss the spaetzli in it, seasoning with more salt and pepper.

POINTS TO WATCH

Countries in which spaetzli is served regularly have developed specific contraptions to do the job. These come in two shapes. The first resembles a frying pan with holes. The second looks like a cheese grater over which a moving cockpit slides to and fro, pushing the batter through the holes and into the boiling water below. An acceptable substitute can be made by jamming a colander over a saucepan of boiling water, or slicing ribbons of the batter on a cutting board, then tilting the board so that they slide into the water.

Whatever method is used, it is important to place only small amounts of batter at a time over the boiling water. The rising steam will otherwise cook the batter in one lump before it has time to reach the water.

FRESH PASTA

Fresh pasta is not superior to dried pasta. They are different products with differing plus and minus points. Fresh is one of those lucky words like 'natural' that instantly produce an aura of goodness, but the fresh in this case is only used in contrast to dried and not as the opposite of 'stale' or even 'frozen'. In fact, fresh pasta freezes very well.

FOR 4 PERSONS

500g (1lb 2oz/3 1/2 cups)
    plain (all-purpose) flour
4 tablespoons olive oil, plus
    extra for cooking
4 medium (large) eggs, plus
    1 yolk
a little grated nutmeg
salt and pepper

Work all the ingredients together and knead for about 5 minutes until shiny. Leave the dough to rest for at least 30 minutes.

Roll out the dough to a manageable thickness, something that will fit into a pasta machine if this is what you are using. Then roll out the dough a further two times to give the desired thinness, allowing the pasta to rest briefly between rollings.

Hang the pasta sheets up to stretch for 30 minutes, then cut them into whatever shape is desired.

To cook, bring a large pan of salted water to the boil and add 1 teaspoon of oil. Add the pasta, cook for 3 minutes, then drain and toss in your chosen sauce.

VARIATIONS

Brightly coloured pasta is achieved by adding ingredients such as spinach or tomato paste. As these are wet, there has to be some reduction in the quantity of egg to compensate. Omitting the extra yolk from this basic recipe will normally do.

Fresh pasta can be deep-fried as well as boiled. Fill it like ravioli with a little cheese or herb stuffing, or twist a piece of pasta like an old style sweetie wrapper, then deep-fry. In Cremona, a town in northern Italy, deep-fried pasta dusted with icing sugar is served as a dessert or with coffee – very nice.

POINTS TO WATCH

A hurdy-gurdy-like machine for rolling pasta is handy but not essential. A rolling pin will produce creditable results.

The dough requires a bit of kneading but is otherwise straightforward. An electric mixer, with dough hook attachment, will save you time.

Roll out the pasta dough in two stages, allowing a short rest in between. This allows the dough to contract slightly. Your aim is have the dough thin.

Whether the dough is machine or hand rolled, it will need stretching. Force of gravity will help if, once the dough is rolled, the pasta is hung for half an hour across a broom handle, rail or similar rod, so that its own weight stretches it.

Once fresh pasta is cooked (the time depends on its thickness but will not be more than a few minutes) it should be drained and served. If it is to be cooled for reheating later, cool it under cold running water, drain, then toss in a few drops of olive oil to stop the strands sticking together. On no account keep cooked pasta in cold water, or it will become brittle and lifeless.

COUSCOUS WITH SPICED VEGETABLES

Couscous is traditionally cooked in the top half of a double saucepan called a couscousière. The idea is that as the stew cooks in the base, the colander-like top section steams the couscous. Presumably this neat system has its origins with nomadic people who may not have carried a fitted kitchen around. In any case, a reasonable substitute may be cobbled together by wedging a sieve on top of your saucepan and stretching kitchen foil across to serve as a lid. My kitchen has room for two pots – just – so I cook the couscous separately in a wide pan. This entails no loss of flavour, and I suggest you splash out on a couscousière only if you intend picnicing in the desert on a regular basis.

FOR 4 PERSONS

FOR THE RAGOÛT

60g (2½oz/½ cup)
  chickpeas (garbanzos)
4 carrots
4 courgettes (zucchini)
1 red bell pepper
2 tablespoons olive oil
8 button onions, peeled
1 teaspoon chopped fresh
  ginger
1 teaspoon paprika
1 heaped teaspoon saffron
4 tablespoons tomato
  passata (sieved tomatoes)
100g (3½oz/¾ cup)
  broad (fava) beans
1 tablespoon chopped fresh
  coriander (cilantro)
1 teaspoon harissa (below)

FOR THE HARISSA

4-5 long thin red chillies
2 cloves garlic
2 teaspoons ground
  coriander
2 teaspoons ground cumin
1 teaspoon fresh mint leaves
2 tablespoons olive oil

FOR THE COUSCOUS

250g (9oz/1½ cups)
  couscous
25g (1oz/¼ stick) butter
a little ground cinnamon
salt

Soak the chickpeas overnight in a generous quantity of water. Next day, boil them in fresh water until tender – this will take about 1 hour.

Meanwhile, to make the harissa, deseeed the chillies and chop them. Soften them in warm water for 5 minutes, then pound them along with the other spices until they form a paste. Whisk in the olive oil.

Cut the carrots, courgettes and bell pepper into 2cm (¾in) slices. Heat the olive oil in a heavy pan and fry the onions until they colour. Sprinkle with ginger, paprika and saffron, then add the passata and chickpeas. Cover with water and bring to the boil.

Add the carrots and simmer for 10 minutes. Add the other vegetables and return the stew to the boil. Let it simmer for a few minutes, then add the coriander leaves.

About 20 minutes before the vegetable stew is ready, put the couscous in a bowl and stir in 250ml (9floz/1 cup) of water. Leave it to absorb for about 15 minutes.

If you are using a couscousière or the sieve and pot arrangement, steam it above the ragoût for about 5 minutes.

To finish, melt the butter in a large frying pan, then add the couscous and heat, stirring continuously. Sprinkle with salt and a little cinnamon to taste. When it's hot, it's ready.

Take a cup of the cooking liquor from the vegetables and whisk in 1 teaspoon of the harissa. Serve the harissa sauce separately in a bowl alongside the couscous and vegetable stew.

POINTS TO WATCH

The vegetables included are a matter of choice and availability.

The fiery spice mixture used is harissa – a recipe is given here but you may well be able to buy it ready made. A mortar and pestle does the job of pounding the chillies and spices effectively. Blenders have trouble with small quantities but will manage if you engage in a little shaking and throttling of the machine to help things along.

If you do not want to steam the couscous, you can put it straight into the frying pan after soaking and it will taste fine.

SAFFRON AND ARTICHOKE RISOTTO

The traditional method of making risotto is to add hot stock frequently, but in small quantities, to the saucepan of cooking rice. Once cooked, it must be served and eaten at once, otherwise residual heat in the risotto means that any liquid continues to be absorbed, overcooking the grains. This useful method allows the cook to prepare at least part of the dish in advance – it works well in restaurant kitchens and allows some flexibility when cooking at home for dinner parties.

FOR 4 PERSONS
4 large globe artichokes
1 tablespoon white wine
1 tablespoon lemon juice
FOR THE RISOTTO
1 tablespoon olive oil
1 tablespoon chopped onion
200g (7oz/scant 1 cup)
* risotto rice*
100ml (3 1/2floz/1/2 cup)
* white wine*
a large pinch of saffron
* threads*
700ml (1 pint 5floz/3 cups)
* chicken stock*
50g (2oz/1/2 cup) grated
* Parmesan cheese*
25g (1oz/1/4 stick) butter
1 tablespoon mixture of
* chopped basil, chives*
* and parsley*
salt and pepper

To prepare the artichokes, snap off and discard the stalks, then trim away the base, sides and leaves as described on page 68.

Bring a pan of salted water to the boil and add the wine. Drop each artichoke heart in the lemon juice and then in the pan. Cover with greaseproof or parchment paper and simmer for 20 minutes or until tender. Leave to cool in the cooking liquid.

To make the risotto, heat the olive oil in a heavy pan and sweat the onion. Add the rice and cook for 3 minutes. Add 1 teaspoon of salt and the wine and let this evaporate completely.

Add the saffron and 225ml (8floz/1 cup) of the stock. Bring to the boil and switch off the heat. Leave the rice to absorb the liquid, which will take about 20 minutes. (After this stage the rice can be left for 1 to 2 days if necessary.)

Fifteen minutes before you want to eat, pour the remaining stock over the rice, stir briefly and simmer until nearly all the liquid has been absorbed.

Quarter the artichokes and stir them into the risotto with the grated cheese, butter and chopped mixed herbs. Leave for 3 to 4 minutes to thicken, then serve.

POINTS TO WATCH
Exact amounts of liquid are of little benefit when making risotto because the speed at which the rice boils will have a substantial effect on the quantity of stock needed. The harder it boils, the more will evaporate rather than be absorbed by the rice, however this absorption technique is somewhat more precise than the traditional method.

There are several varieties of risotto rice available in the stores now. Arborio, carnaroli and vialone nano are all suitable for this dish.

Fish and shellfish

Chefs love cooking fish, especially white fish like sole or turbot. It responds well to the cook's art in ways that meat does not and can be treated with endless permutations of wine and herbs, with butter, cream or olive oil. It's a shame, then, that it isn't especially popular, except as a first course bridesmaid to the main course meat. Few people think of having a sea bass or cod as the centrepiece to a grand meal.

When buying seafood, the best approach is to choose a particular type – white fish, shell-fish or whatever – and shop flexibly within that category. Strict adherence to recipes that call for uncommon varieties can be frustrating if the main ingredient is scarce. Treatments of an oily fish like mackerel, for instance, will probably suit herring if that is fresher or cheaper on the day. Ditto cod and haddock or turbot and brill.

Certainly fish is so scarce and expensive that it must be regarded as a luxury and treated with some respect. There are very few bargains in prime fish such as sole or bass. In Britain, prices aren't dictated by supply and demand alone (if so they would be cheaper) but by prices across Europe. As you are going to pay a high price for anything other than miserable farmed specimens, it is best to search out something in peak condition – firm fleshed with sparkling skin. Avoid those that seem like they are too long away from the ocean or have paid a visit to the freezer – tired, lifeless and dry looking.

Have your fishmonger clean and fillet the fish. For emergencies – someone has triumphantly returned from a fishing trip perhaps and wants their trout prepared for breakfast – a rundown of filleting procedures is included here. Remember the last water a fish should see before cooking is the ocean or stream whence it came. Water dries out fish, leaving it less tender. If the fish needs cleaning, do it swiftly, drying afterwards with paper towels. If it's

The last water a fish should see before cooking is the ocean or stream.

not practical to buy what you need on the day of cooking, wrap your purchase well and store it on the bottom shelf of the refrigerator so that nothing drips down onto other food.

Any delicate cooking method suits seafood and overcooking is the enemy. Even uncooked fish dishes such as gravadlax or ceviche will suffer if salted or marinated too long. To test whether the fish is cooked, press your finger gently against the thickest part. If there is any feeling of springiness, like a rubber ball, it needs more cooking. Fish cooked on the bone is easier to judge for it will only part company with the bone when completely done. If you want to deliberately undercook a piece of fish, salmon or tuna perhaps, take it off the bone first.

Cleaning and filleting fish

If you are obliged to clean and fillet fish a number of times, your speed will improve with the practice. Begin by cutting off anything that protrudes, fins and suchlike. Scale those fish that have them. Scrape the knife at right angles to the fish, from tail to head. Scales will fly everywhere, so try not to work next to your bread or dessert.

For round fish, slit the belly and take out the innards. This is not a job for the squeamish. Rinse with cold water, then dry thoroughly. If you want to cook the fish on the bone, this is as much as you need do. If you intend filleting, then continue like this:

Cut off the head. Lay the fish on its side, then cut the skin along the spinal edge. Hold the fish steady with the flat of your hand and carefully cut away the fillet. Turn the fish over and repeat. This should leave you with two fillets. Use tweezers to pull out the line of pin bones that run the length of each fillet.

For flat specimens, skin the fish by making a cut across the tail, below the point where the flesh ends, enough to sever the skin but not chop off the tail completely. Raise a corner of the skin away from the bone and grasp it tightly between thumb and forefinger. Pull the skin back and away from the meat – with luck it will come away in one movement. Repeat the operation on the other side. As you pull away the skin with your right hand, keep the fish firmly in place by holding it steady with your left hand.

Move your finger along the centre of the fish from head to tail. The ridge of bone dividing the two fillets will be obvious. Cut downwards along this line, sliding the knife under the fillets and across to the side. The framework of bones will keep you from cutting too deeply, so keep your knife angled downwards away from expensive flesh and vulnerable fingers. Work from head to tail, taking as much time as you need.

WARM TEA-SMOKED TROUT

Smoking is essentially a controlled form of tainting food. Those with a taste for kippers and hot-smoked salmon may like to experiment with this method before investing in a home smoke box for their personalized smoked garlic (nice), bloaters (quite nice) or lamb (not nice at all), all of which can be bought at a premium price in fancy shops these days.

Hot tea smoking is easy and requires no special equipment. The technique bears a strong resemblance to steaming, with pressure from hot smoke cooking and flavouring the fish in just a few minutes. Differences in the tea used and the temperatures reached will affect the final flavour. With a little modification, this treatment also suits larger and more firmly textured fish. For example, monkfish cut into slices and brushed with grapefruit juice produces a fine result.

FOR 4 PERSONS

4 medium trout

1 tablespoon lemon juice

*1 tablespoon light sesame
   oil*

*3 tablespoons black
   China tea*

3 tablespoons uncooked rice

2 tablespoons brown sugar

salt and pepper

Fillet the fish or – better – have someone else fillet it. Brush the fillets with the lemon juice and sesame oil, then season with salt and pepper.

Line the bottom of a wok or other deep pan with a folded square of kitchen foil and put in the tea, rice and sugar.

Place the fish on a steamer, wire rack or trivet above the tea mixture. Seal with a tight fitting lid, or more foil.

Cook at a high heat for 5 minutes, then switch off the heat and leave the wok unopened for 20 minutes.

Serve with a salad dressed with a little sesame oil and lemon.

POINTS TO WATCH

A wok is ideal but any saucepan or deep frying pan can be drafted in for the job, providing it is wide enough to hold a metal rack and deep enough for the smoke to rise and circulate.

   Choose a mild China tea such as keemun. Smoked tea such as lapsang souchong will, perversely, give too powerful a taste.

   Whole trout may be used if you prefer. Have the fishmonger clean and gut them and double the cooking time given here.

MACKEREL WITH INDIAN SPICES, LIME AND DHAL

Sauces like this that would kill the subtlety of white fish such as sole or plaice can work well with robust specimens like mackerel and herring. This particular one has evolved from a strong Indian masala to a spicy, citrusy concoction that counters the rich oiliness of the mackerel beautifully. It's best served with something of contrasting texture, a crisp green salad perhaps or the carrot fritters (page 74).

FOR 4 PERSONS

30g (1oz/2 tablespoons)
  brown or green lentils
1 small onion, chopped
2 cloves garlic, chopped
1 small chilli, deseeded and
  chopped
a knob of fresh ginger,
  peeled and chopped
vegetable oil, for frying
1 teaspoon ground
  cardamom
1 teaspoon ground
  cinnamon
1 teaspoon ground cumin
150ml (5floz/3/4 cup) fish
  stock or water
1 tablespoon lime juice
2 tablespoons coriander
  (cilantro) leaves
1 tablespoon chopped
  chives
8 small or 4 large mackerel

Boil the lentils until tender, then drain and set aside until needed.

Fry the onion, garlic, chilli and ginger in vegetable oil until brown, then add the spices and fry for a few seconds more. Add the stock or water and the lentils and simmer for 20 minutes.

Purée the sauce using a food mill or blender. Reheat, adding the lime juice, coriander leaves and chives. Check the seasoning for balance and keep the sauce warm.

In a large pan, fry the mackerel on each side until done. Make a pool of sauce on each plate, place the fish on top and serve.

POINTS TO WATCH

Indian spices must fry for a few seconds or they will taste raw (like a Frenchman's curry) no matter how long they are cooked afterwards.

Slash the mackerels' skin diagonally on each side before cooking. It's not necessary to fillet the fish in this case.

MONKFISH WITH MUSTARD AND CUCUMBER

Here the cucumber is salted and pressed for 2 hours to extract the juices, then squeezed and mixed with a sweet-sour dressing of vinegar and sugar. The resulting salad is a standard accompaniment to gulyas or any rich stew in Hungary. It works well in this dish for the same reason, to cut through and balance the creaminess of the sauce. This is equally good as a first or main course.

FOR 4 PERSONS

1 small cucumber

1 tablespoon caster (granulated) sugar

1 tablespoon white wine vinegar

1 teaspoon freshly ground black pepper

125ml (4floz/1/2 cup) fish stock

1 tablespoon double (heavy) cream

1 tablespoon wholegrain mustard

50g (2oz/1/2 stick) unsalted butter, plus extra for frying

1 teaspoon lemon juice

4 monkfish tails, about 200g (7oz) each

sunflower oil, for brushing

salt

Peel and thinly slice the cucumber. Mix it with 1 teaspoon of salt and press for 2 hours – placing a small plate and a full jar of marmalade or similar on top will do the job.

In a separate bowl, mix together the sugar, vinegar and pepper. Squeeze as much liquid as you can from the cucumber and toss the slices in the sweet and sour dressing.

Make the sauce by bringing the stock, cream and mustard to a boil then whisking in the butter to thicken. Season with a few drops of lemon juice.

Paint the monkfish fillets with oil and fry in a hot, dry pan until sealed. Add a knob of butter to the pan and continue to fry until done. Squeeze a few drops of lemon juice over the monkfish.

Place the cooked fish onto warm plates, then add the pickled cucumber and, finally, the sauce.

POINTS TO WATCH

Monkfish is unusual among fish in that the smaller specimens are preferable to the larger. The texture of large monkfish is hard and muscular and eating them can feel like eating biceps, whereas smaller ones are almost crustacean-like in taste and texture. Fish dealers have fortunately not caught on and so the smaller monkfish are considerably less expensive than the older ones.

Fishmongers invariably leave monkfish untrimmed. Cut away the membrane-like inner skin and you will see a line from head to tail along the centre of the flesh. There is no bone there but the fish will cook more evenly if you gently slice along the line, to about halfway down the fillet, and open it up.

Fish stock is not central to the success of this sauce and can be replaced by chicken stock or even by a mixture of dry sherry and water if this suits you better.

The butter can be replaced by olive oil providing the sauce is then puréed in a blender. This will give a cleaner taste.

COD IN BEER BATTER

The traditional grease-up holds real nostalgia value for those of us who grew up in Britain before the burger and pizza chains took hold, but it's a pity about the offerings generally available. People tend not to want to order battered cod in restaurants and, to be perfectly honest, we don't serve this to customers at The Merchant House, we cook and eat it ourselves. Chips are the obvious accompaniment but another possibility is something light and fresh like a green salad.

Deep-frying with any success is dependent on the use of decent oil at the right temperature, fresh fish and an interesting coating of batter. The batter is there to protect the fish during cooking as well as to give a crunchy contrast afterwards. Most batters call for a raising agent in the flour otherwise they will be heavy and dull. The ultra-light batter used for tempura relies on egg and chilled water but baking powder, or self-raising flour, will also do the trick. Similarly, yeast or whisked egg whites folded in at the last moment will give the necessary lightness.

FOR 4 PERSONS

4 cod fillets, about 200g
   (7oz) each
sunflower oil, for deep-frying
FOR THE BATTER
150ml (5floz/2/3 cup) beer
125g (41/2oz/1 cup)
   self-raising (self-rising) flour
1 tablespoon olive oil
2 egg whites
salt

To make the batter, mix together the beer, flour, olive oil and a little salt. In a separate bowl, whisk the egg whites until stiff, then fold them into the batter.

Heat the sunflower oil in a wok or other large pan suitable for deep-frying. Working in batches, dip the fish fillets in the batter and slide them into the hot oil. The fish will rise to the surface when cooked. Lift out, drain on paper towels and serve hot.

POINTS TO WATCH

Batter has a tendency to fly away from the fish when dropped in hot oil. If you have doubts about its sticking power, dust the fish finely with flour before dipping in the batter.

In this particular recipe, the right temperature for the oil is 190°C (375°F), but you can fry smaller pieces of fish at higher temperatures.

Don't fry too much at one time. A whole batch of fish will cause a swift reduction in oil temperature and the fish will absorb a lot of oil by the time the temperature has recovered.

Never leave heating oil unattended, it's a major cause of accidents. Should the pan catch fire, place a cloth across the top to smother the flames (with no gaps for oxygen to enter) and turn off the heat.

JOHN DORY WITH SAUERKRAUT AND JUNIPER SABAYON

The idea for this dish is pinched from Le Crocodil restaurant in Strasbourg. Anja and I ate there with my brother and his wife, who live not far away in Basel. I had booked the table using Relais and Châteaux headed notepaper (at the time I worked at Gidleigh Park which was a member), so we received personal attention from the chef-patron. We were seated at chairs used the previous week to accommodate Mrs Thatcher's bottom and the patron politely asked my brother what brought him to the area. In those days my brother was a garbage man and the conversation took a humorous turn as he explained to the incredulous owner that we weren't as refined and august as it might appear. Madame wasn't surprised as she had assessed our scruffy clothes and car earlier. The meal, however, was quite brilliant.

Le Crocodil's version employs zander, a freshwater fish caught locally but one that's actually rather dull because it hasn't been to sea. I use john dory because it's firm enough to balance the creamy sauce and strong enough to match the sauerkraut, which is important even though not much is used.

FOR 4 PERSONS

*2 large or 4 small john dory,
  about 1kg (2lb 4oz) in
  total*
4 tablespoons sauerkraut
*50ml (2floz/1/4 cup) white
  wine*
1 tablespoon juniper berries
3 egg yolks
1 tablespoon lemon juice
a dash of Tabasco sauce
1 teaspoon chopped chives
*1 teaspoon finely chopped
  carrots*
salt

Fillet the fish or have this done for you. Place 1/2 to 1 tablespoon of sauerkraut on top of each fillet, depending on whether you have 8 or 4 pieces. Steam for 5 to 8 minutes or until cooked.

Meanwhile, heat the wine and juniper berries together gently. In a rounded pan or a bowl suspended over hot water, whisk the egg yolks and juniper-flavoured wine together over a low heat to give a sabayon – the yolks will thicken as they cook and the volume of sauce will almost double. Season the sabayon with lemon juice, Tabasco sauce and salt.

Scatter the chives and chopped carrot around the plates then lay the steamed fish and sauerkraut at the centre of each. Spoon the sabayon on top and serve immediately.

POINTS TO WATCH

John dory are miserable-looking creatures with large heads and vicious spines. Unusually for white fish, there is only one fillet per side. Fillet them by cutting along the sides of the spine and then sliding the knife between fillet and bone. Keep the bones – they make good stock.

John dory is firm-textured but not particularly thick, so it will cook quickly.

Sauerkraut is fermented cabbage. It's always been a bit of a joke and serves as a term of abuse for anyone whose native tongue is German. It's worth remembering however, that sauerkraut is meant to taste pleasant, not be an ordeal, so if it is salty or bitter, rinse it in some warm water.

Juniper berries are usually quite soft but can, if stored too long, dry up and harden. They will still give plenty of flavour in this condition but are then best discarded rather than served in the sabayon sauce.

GRILLED SEA BASS WITH BASIL AND CRÈME FRAÎCHE

FOR 4 PERSONS

150ml (5floz/2/3 cup) fish
  stock
1 shallot, chopped
25g (1oz/1/4 stick) unsalted
  butter
1 tablespoon crème fraîche
1 tablespoon lemon juice
a few drops of Tabasco
  sauce
100ml (3 1/2floz/7 table-
  spoons) olive oil
50g (2oz/2 cups) basil
25g (1oz/1 cup) flat-leaf
  parsley
1/2 teaspoon lemon zest
1 small clove garlic, crushed
4 fillets sea bass, about
  175g (6oz) each
salt and black pepper

Warm the stock, chopped shallot, butter and crème fraîche
together. Purée in a blender, then season with lemon juice,
Tabasco sauce and salt. Return to the saucepan and set aside.

In the blender, combine the olive oil, basil, parsley, lemon zest,
garlic and some freshly ground black pepper and set aside.

Grill or broil the sea bass, skin-side up only, until done.

Reheat the pan of stock mixture and gradually whisk in the basil
oil to give a creamy sauce. Serve the bass on a pool of sauce.

SKATE WITH LEMON, CAPERS AND MUSTARD

FOR 4 PERSONS

4 small-to-medium skate
  wings, about 1kg (2lb 4oz)
  in total
1 tablespoon lemon
  juice
50ml (2floz/1/4 cup) fish
  stock
50ml (2floz/1/4 cup) crème
  fraîche
1 tablespoon dry vermouth
1 tablespoon Dijon mustard
1 tablespoon capers
1 tablespoon chopped
  parsley
salt and pepper

Season the skate with some salt and place the fish, on a plate,
in a steamer. Steam for around 10 minutes or until done – test
the thickest corner, the meat should lift away from the cartilage.
Sprinkle the fish with a little lemon juice.

Pour any liquor that has gathered on the plate into a small
saucepan. Add the stock, crème fraîche, vermouth, mustard and
capers. Bring to the boil, stirring continuously. Add a little lemon
juice and the parsley, then pour the sauce around the fish.

GRILLED SEA BASS WITH BASIL AND CRÈME FRAÎCHE

The difficulty with a new restaurant is that no one knows quite what to expect. People might read that a good restaurant has opened but find that their own definition of excellence differs radically from that of the reviewer or the restaurateur. The opening months can have awkward moments while people, some of whom like the style and some of whom do not, pay a visit. There is an element of natural selection at work, and if there are not enough yes votes in the form of return visits, the restaurant will be in trouble.

Our outlook was simple: we would spend much more than the usual percentage of the menu price on food and wine so that there need be no skimping on quality ingredients, and we would compensate by employing a minimum of staff. This meant that fine Cornish lobster and sea bass could be on the menu, but we would be washing pots at the end of each evening rather than hobnobbing with the customers. It also meant that once the chosen wine was opened and tasted, people would be left to fill their own glasses.

These so-called drawbacks suited me for I'm not convinced that everyone wants the chef coming around fishing for compliments at the end of the meal, nor do I want anyone to pour my wine. Our gamble was that there would be enough people in agreement to make The Merchant House a success. An article in the *Guardian* newspaper in advance of our opening and coverage in a key trade magazine meant that the telephone started ringing and, for the first few weeks at least, we attracted both the curious and the competition.

WARM OYSTERS WITH CHAMP AND CAVIAR

Native British oysters are the flat ones that cost a lot. They are best eaten raw and are found only in the winter months. Rock oysters are cheaper and more readily available, whatever the season. They aren't as thrilling to eat raw, however, and need a little help to taste interesting.

Champ is an Irish potato dish, consisting of mashed potato beaten with lots of milk and butter then chopped spring onion. It serves a dual purpose here, acting as a starchy contrast to the oysters and butter sauce, and as docking device into which the shells may be fastened.

FOR 4 PERSONS

16 rock oysters

4 teaspoons caviar, optional

FOR THE CHAMP

400g (14oz) old potatoes

2 tablespoons warm milk

25g (1oz/¼ stick) unsalted butter

6 spring onions (scallions), chopped

salt and pepper

FOR THE SAUCE

2 tablespoons white wine

1 shallot, chopped

100g (3½oz/7 tablespoons) unsalted butter, cubed

1 tablespoon chopped chives

1 teaspoon lemon juice

Shuck the oysters and keep them in a bowl for later. Scrub the shells and boil them in plenty of water until thoroughly cleaned.

To make the champ, peel and boil the potatoes until tender. Drain and mash them, then beat in the milk, butter and spring onions. Season with plenty of salt and pepper.

For the sauce, boil the wine and shallot together in a saucepan. When the volume of liquid has reduced by half, whisk in the butter, piece by piece, so that it thickens into a sauce. Season with the chives, lemon juice and some salt.

Place a dollop of champ in the centre of each serving plate. Push 4 hot shells into the champ on each plate, then slip an oyster into each shell. Top with the sauce and caviar, if using.

POINTS TO WATCH

The oysters are not really cooked, just slipped back into hot boiled shells and covered with a warm butter sauce. This heats them enough for the dish.

Caviar is not improved by prolonged contact with heat. If you are adding this luxury to the dish (it is good but not as exciting without it) then take care to place it on the dish at the last moment.

The mashed potato is made with maincrop or old potatoes. Smart places often use new potatoes or waxy varieties like Ratte, Charlotte or Yukon Gold for their mash. The idea is that such densely textured spuds will absorb much more butter, so giving a richer end product, but that's not necessary here.

Preparing a lobster

There are several schools of thought on the most humane method of despatching lobsters. My preference is to drop them into a pot of boiling water (an instant exit for them) and then simmer for 9 to 10 minutes per 1kg (2lb 4oz) of lobster.

To dismantle the cooked lobster you need a pair of kitchen scissors, a pair of rubber gloves and a small bowl to catch the juice and coral. First break the tail from the body. Scoop out the coral from the main body shell (this is a powerful dye, so wear the gloves and scrub the work surface well afterwards).

Use scissors to cut along the underside of the tail. You should be able to easily release the whole tail in one piece. Break off the claws and discard the carapace. Twist the pincers from the claws – these will pull out a length of hard membrane from the claw meat at the same time. Break off the two arm joints that are attached.

Using the blunt side of a heavy knife, tap each claw to crack it, then lift out the meat. Use a skewer or similar device to pick the remaining meat from the arm joints.

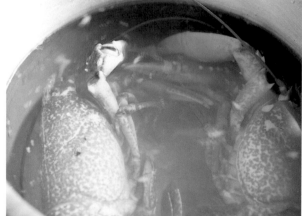

LOBSTER WITH CHICKPEA, CORIANDER AND OLIVE OIL SAUCE

This hummus-like sauce is related in concept to the lentil dhal that partners mackerel in an earlier recipe. The sauce's subdued spiciness contrasts well with the sweetness in the lobster and, though the presentation is simple, care has to be taken at every stage for the dish to reach its full potential.

Lobster loses its sweetness if refrigerated for any length of time after cooking – that's why cold lobster is so regularly a disappointment – so this dish must be cooked and eaten the same day. However it can be prepared in advance to a certain extent and the sauce may be made whenever you fancy.

FOR 4 PERSONS

2 lobsters, 600g (1lb 5oz)
    each
1 tablespoon salt
1 tablespoon vinegar

FOR THE SAUCE

100g (3 1/2oz/1/2 cup)
    chickpeas (garbanzos),
    soaked overnight in water
4 shallots, chopped
2 cloves garlic, chopped
1 teaspoon ground cinnamon
1 teaspoon ground coriander
1 teaspoon ground cumin
1 lemon
200ml (7floz/3/4 cup) fish
    stock
200ml (7floz/3/4 cup) olive
    oil, plus extra for frying
1 tablespoon coriander
    (cilantro) leaves
1 tablespoon chopped chives
salt

Boil the soaked chickpeas in fresh water for about 1 hour or until they are very tender.

Fry the shallot and garlic in a little olive oil until cooked but not coloured. Add the spices, a slice of the lemon, and the chickpeas. Pour in the stock and cook gently for 30 minutes.

Purée the chickpea mixture in a blender with the olive oil, lemon juice and some salt.

To cook the lobsters, bring a large pan of water to the boil. Add the salt and vinegar to acidulate the water. Boil the lobsters for 10 minutes, then refresh them in cold water.

Take the meat from the shells as per the instructions on page 108 and divide into four portions. Reheat the lobster meat briefly in warm cooking liquor if necessary.

Just before serving, add the fresh herbs to the chickpea sauce. Serve the portions of lobster on pools of the sauce.

POINTS TO WATCH

Lobsters are prone to become a health hazard if left in the warm for any length of time, which is a key reason why it is best to despatch them yourself.

It is okay to boil the lobsters and shell them an hour or so ahead of time, but you must never re-boil the meat or even put it in very hot stock. I keep a little of the cooking liquor and all the coral and trimmings from the shells and heat this to the temperature of a warm bath. Then, when the dish is to be assembled, I turn off the heat and place the lobster meat in the hot broth for a few minutes to warm through. Any hotter and the lobster meat will become tense and tough.

The coral will still be dark green when you begin dismantling the lobster but may have started to change colour to the deep red it becomes when fully cooked. Remember, it can stain almost everything. It can also be used in seafood sauces.

Should you be thinking of cooking lobster on a regular basis, there is a small piece of cutlery available designed to assist you in removing the remnants of meat from the claws.

Poultry

Poultry has regularly served as the centrepiece to important meals: in medieval times, peacock or swan was the favourite and nowadays, at Christmas, a turkey or goose. Restaurants rarely suit this sort of occasion. When a chef sends out three slices of white turkey breast on a plate next to some cranberries or sage and onion stuffing, it does not have quite the same impact as the grand banquet with lots of carving at the table and passing of the port.

Similarly, a good-size turkey will take three hours to cook and needs a family of eight committed to its consumption. Smaller birds fill the restaurant's requirements far better. Indeed, those with white meat, like partridge or guinea fowl, positively benefit from the cook's art for they can be dry and dull if simply roasted at too high a temperature or without generous helpings of butter and oil basted over them while cooking. Wild duck breasts can be treated almost like steak, cooked quickly and served underdone, making them ideal for restaurants.

Birds have evolved for reasons other than gastronomic pleasure.

Their bloodied flavour is completely different to that of the deliciously fatty Aylesbury breed, which needs to be cooked right through.

Birds have evolved into their current shape and strength for reasons other than gastronomic pleasure or ease of cooking. Consequently, there is no reason why legs – designed to cart the rest of the body around the fields or farmyard floor – should be as tender or, more importantly, cook at the same speed as breasts, which have been passengers in the previous arrangement. The nearer to wild the bird, the more this applies and, once you arrive at wild duck and pheasant, for instance, it is best to remove the legs and cook them separately. Best of all is to braise or confit them ahead of time so that their full flavour comes through and the gelatinous, sinewy dark meat turns into something that is different from, but entirely complementary to, the just-cooked breast.

Good quality poultry, decently fed and reared, is not much more expensive than the intensively produced rubbish and the results are immeasurably superior. A chicken that is to be roasted or poached rather than submerged in spices or coated with breadcrumbs needs to be free range, and preferably organic, to taste of anything worthwhile.

Remember too that raw poultry should be handled with care as the dangers of cross-contamination are higher than for other meats. Do not cut up a raw chicken or duck on the same work surface on which you are to cut up anything that has already been cooked without scrubbing between uses. The same goes for any knife used.

ROAST CHICKEN WITH GRAVY AND WATERCRESS STUFFING

If the same effort that is put into complicated dishes is directed towards cooking something simple, the results can be a revelation. Here is a good example: free range chicken, carefully roasted so that the thighs are completely cooked but the breasts not overdone, and a sauce made from pan juices and roasting tray residues rather than commercial bouillon cubes or gravy mixes.

FOR 4 PERSONS

1.75kg (3lb 14oz) chicken
2 tablespoons olive oil
1 tablespoon butter
1 clove garlic, crushed
1 tablespoon chervil
1 teaspoon tomato passata
(sieved tomatoes)
salt and pepper

FOR THE STUFFING

25g (1oz/2 tablespoons)
ready-to-eat dried apricots
1 shallot, chopped
25g (1oz/1/4 stick) butter
4 tablespoons fresh
breadcrumbs
4 tablespoons chopped
watercress
25g (1oz/1/4 cup) ground
hazelnuts

To make the stuffing, heat the apricots in 1 tablespoon of water for a few minutes, then chop them. Sweat the chopped shallot in the butter. Place the remaining stuffing ingredients in a bowl, add the apricots, then the shallot and butter in which it cooked. Mix well. Roll into a sausage shape and wrap in kitchen foil.

Heat the oven to 220°C (425°F/Gas 7). Remove the chicken's wishbone. Paint the bird with olive oil, then the butter, being generous. Season with salt and pepper and rub with the crushed garlic and chervil.

Place the chicken in a roasting tray with 100ml (3 1/2floz/1/2 cup) of water. Roast for 15 minutes, then lower the temperature to 190°C (375°F/Gas 5) and continue roasting the chicken for another 50 minutes. Halfway through cooking, turn the bird upside down to help the thighs cook properly. Baste with pan juices and add the stuffing to the roasting tray at that point.

Take the chicken from the oven and leave it in the roasting tray to rest for 10 minutes. Carve the chicken into breasts and legs, then halve each piece. Pour any juices that escape from the bird back into the roasting tray.

Skim half the fat from the roasting tray, leaving the remainder to flavour and thicken the gravy. Add the tomato passata and 400ml (14floz/1 3/4 cups) of water. Bring the mixture to the boil, whisking, then strain the gravy into a sauceboat for serving with the chicken and its stuffing.

POINTS TO WATCH

Test the chicken to see whether it is done by piercing the thigh and then watching whether the juices that escape are clear, meaning cooked, or pink, meaning underdone.

Beware of tomato purée (paste). A tiny amount will give body and a deeper colour to the gravy, but too much will overpower any chicken flavour. Tomato passata (sieved tomatoes), which is not a concentrate, is a better option. You could use a scant teaspoonful of tomato purée instead, but it will need to cook for a while, so should be added while the roasting tray is still very hot.

Gravy from chicken will never be as dark as that from roast lamb or beef. Remember it does not matter if the gravy is light in colour, it only matters if it does not taste good.

Chicken gravy is generally left thin. It can be thickened in the same way as beef gravy by sprinkling a teaspoon of flour onto the roasting tray, letting it cook a minute, then stirring in the water. This mixture will then need to be sieved. Alternatively, some potato flour (fécule) can be whisked into the liquid and boiled to thicken the gravy.

POACHED CHICKEN WITH SUMMER HERBS

White meat is well suited to poaching. On a summer day poached chicken will make a fine one-pot meal. The vegetables simmer alongside the meat and the cooking liquor provides the basis for a classy sauce. Use a good roasting chicken – don't buy anything labelled boiling fowl as this indicates an older bird, worn out from intensive laying. The selection of vegetables given here is just a guideline: use whatever is freshest and best on the day.

FOR 4 PERSONS

1.5kg (3lb 6oz) chicken
12 small new potatoes,
  scraped
100g (3 1/2oz/2/3 cup)
  runner (green) beans
100g (3 1/2oz/2/3 cup)
  broad (fava) beans
4 baby courgettes (zucchini)
8 baby carrots
50g (2oz/1/3 cup) fresh
  peas
100g (3 1/2oz/7 tablespoons)
  unsalted butter
2 egg yolks
1 tablespoon crème fraîche
1 teaspoon lemon juice
1 tablespoon chopped basil
1 tablespoon chopped chervil
1 tablespoon chopped chives
salt and pepper

Measure out just enough cold water to cover the chicken and heat it in your chosen pot. When the water comes to the boil, add a pinch of salt, then the chicken and new potatoes. Cover and poach until done – this will take around 40 minutes depending on the size of the chicken.

Meanwhile, prepare the vegetables: destring the runner beans and cut them into thin strips, pod the broad beans and peel off the inner skins, halve the courgettes lengthways. Melt the butter in a small pan and set aside until needed.

Lift the chicken and potatoes out onto a dish. Add the other vegetables to the cooking liquor in the order in which they take to cook: carrots first, then runner beans, and finally broad beans, courgettes and peas. If the vegetables are young, they will take no more than 3 to 4 minutes in total. Lift the cooked vegetables from the stock and place on a dish.

Take 50ml (2floz/1/4 cup) of the cooking liquor and place it in a small saucepan. Add the egg yolks and whisk over a low heat. When the yolks begin to thicken, whisk in the melted butter a little at a time so that it thickens like a hollandaise sauce.

Add the crème fraîche, lemon juice, salt and pepper, then whisk in enough of the remaining hot cooking liquor as needed to thin the sauce. At the last moment, add the fresh herbs.

Carve the chicken into two breast and leg portions. Cut each breast into two and joint the legs into thighs and drumsticks. Divide these and the vegetables between four warmed plates, then spoon over the sauce.

POINTS TO WATCH

Archimedes' principle is important when cooking the chicken. You want to use the least possible water so the stock is well flavoured. Choosing the right sized pot is important for the same reason. Test the quantity of water in advance with cold water and raw chicken.

A 1.5kg (3lb 6oz) chicken will take 40 minutes to cook. This timing assumes that the water was at boiling point when the chicken was added and that the pot had been covered with a lid. Try not to let the chicken boil as this will make the meat dry. Simmering is the ideal.

Be sparing when salting the water in which the chicken cooks, as it will be used later when making the sauce.

Remove the wishbone from the chicken before cooking. Carving will be easier without it.

Lift the chicken from its stock with either slotted spoons or a long-pronged fork. If using a fork, skewer the bird across the backbone and below the breast meat. This gives you plenty of control and does not dig holes in the flesh.

Remember that the central cavity of the chicken will be full of liquid. Tip the bird slightly as you take it from the pot to let this liquor run back.

LEMON CHICKEN

On a gastronomic trip to Morocco, I ate a version of this dish every evening for four days as successive smart restaurants offered it up on their set menus. It was good enough to withstand this – just. Preserved lemons can be bought in supermarkets now but are easy enough to make if you think about it in advance. Bores who worry about things being authentic will tell you that whole lemons must be used and that months must pass by before use. Just humour them. Life's too short.

FOR 4 PERSONS
1.5kg (3lb 6oz) chicken
1 medium onion, chopped
1 teaspoon ground
  cinnamon
1 teaspoon ground cumin
1 teaspoon ground ginger
1 teaspoon paprika
1 heaped teaspoon saffron
  threads
100ml (3 1/2 floz/1/3 cup)
  chicken stock or water
50g (2oz/1/3 cup) cooked
  chickpeas (garbanzos)
50g (2oz/1/3 cup) pitted
  green olives
the rind from 1 preserved
  lemon (see below)
2 tablespoons chopped
  coriander (cilantro)
1 tablespoon chopped
  parsley
olive oil, for frying
FOR THE PRESERVED LEMONS
12 lemons
150g (5oz/1/2 cup) salt

To make the preserved lemons, cut half the lemons into six wedges each and toss in the salt. Place in a jar. Juice the remaining lemons, pour into the jar, making sure the wedges are covered, and leave for a week before use.

Joint the chicken into breasts, thighs and drumsticks. Fry the onion in a little oil until it starts to colour. Add the chicken pieces and cook until coloured on each side.

Lift the pan away from direct heat and add the spices. Cook for 1 minute. Add the stock or water, return the pan to the heat and bring to the boil. Add the chickpeas and olives, reduce the heat and simmer for 45 minutes.

Finely chop the preserved lemon rind, discarding the flesh. Stir it into the chicken along with the fresh herbs, then serve.

POINTS TO WATCH
The spices need to be added to the pan when it is off the heat to prevent them burning.

The cooking liquid will reduce considerably while the chicken is simmering. Should the pan become too dry, add some more stock or water.

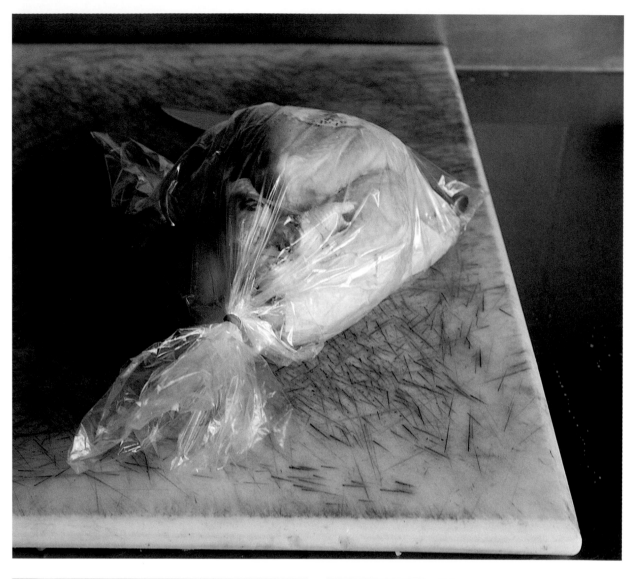

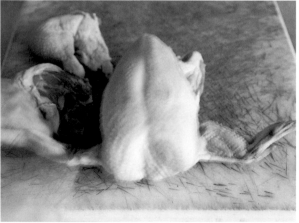

Jointing a chicken

Dismantling a chicken is straightforward providing the job is done in the correct order and you remember to cut out the wishbone. The wishbone makes carving the cooked chicken difficult as well and needs removing even if you are roasting or poaching the bird whole.

Cut off the winglets at the elbow joint. Lift each leg back and away from the body until the bone snaps from its socket. This should now cut away quite easily. You can divide each leg in two by cutting across the thigh and drumstick.

Lift up the flap of skin surrounding the neck. The wishbone forms an arch around the cavity and can be cut out with little loss of breast meat.

Use a small sharp knife rather than any heavy chopping implement to follow the line along and to each side of the breast bone. Cut downwards and keep the knife next to the breastbone until the fillet comes right away. If you need bone attached to the breast meat (perhaps to keep the meat stretched while cooking) then use a heavier knife and cut straight down along the breast bone, splitting the carcass.

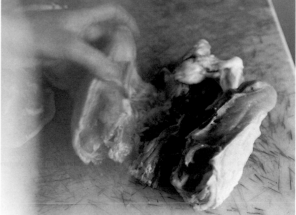

BOURRIDE OF CHICKEN

I have been using this recipe for years and cannot remember where it originates. I saw the idea in a book called *Secrets of the Great French Restaurants* by Louisette Bertholle sometime around 1970 but have no recollection which 'great French restaurant' was credited. The recipe has in any case mutated over the years to the point of being similar only in its basic concept.

Bourride is a fish soup thickened with garlic mayonnaise and this version using chicken copies the principle. You can cook and present the chicken whole if you prefer. For reasons of time and practicality in the restaurant, I make one portion at a time with the chicken jointed but left on the bone, and cook some potatoes and leeks in with the bird.

FOR 4 PERSONS

1.5kg (3lb 6oz) chicken
1/2 small red bell pepper
1/2 small chilli, deseeded
2cm (3/4in) strip of lemon
    rind
8 small or 4 large new
    potatoes
1 heaped teaspoon saffron
    threads
a pinch of ground cumin
4 small leeks

FOR THE GARLIC MAYONNAISE

6 cloves garlic, crushed
2 egg yolks
1 tablespoon white wine
    vinegar
1 teaspoon Dijon mustard
50ml (2floz/1/4 cup)
    sunflower oil
50ml (2floz/1/4 cup) olive oil
salt and pepper

Divide the chicken into breast, leg and thigh portions. In a heavy lidded pot or casserole, fry the chicken, bell pepper, chilli and lemon rind until they start to colour.

Add 500ml (18floz/2 1/4 cups) of water, then the potatoes, saffron and cumin. Bring to the boil. Cover and cook either on top of the stove for 20 minutes, or in a 200°C (400°F/Gas 6) oven.

Lift the chicken out from the pot and carve. If it is still slightly underdone, put it back in the pot for a few moments.

Add the leeks to the potatoes in the pot and bring to the boil.

To make the garlic mayonnaise, whisk together the garlic, egg yolks, vinegar and mustard, then slowly whisk in the oils.

Remove the potatoes and leeks from the cooking liquid. Take the meat from the drumsticks and any other trimmings and purée them in a blender with the cooking liquid, which will have reduced in volume by about one-third.

Add the garlic mayonnaise, a teaspoonful at a time, to the blender until the mixture is the texture of a light sauce. Taste and adjust the seasoning as necessary, then serve with the chicken and vegetables.

There is a lot of inspecting done at the smart end of the restaurant trade. This can be wonderful free publicity that boosts morale more than anything sensible like a tax rebate, or, if the tone of the review is negative, it can be seriously depressing.

Those who claim indifference to the stars, marks, gongs or whatever is allocated by the restaurant guides and magazines are not necessarily to be believed. Personal remarks about your taste and comparative judgements between your efforts and those of your competitors strike deep. Then there is the Schadenfreude: a demotion in the *Good Food Guide* or a negative review would bring joy to those in the trade who are big on envy but low on talent, and we couldn't have that, could we? So we have to try hard.

Most restaurant staff usually do not recognize reviewers and inspectors and are better for it. My system, in previous kitchens, if I thought a food guide inspector was eating, was always to keep the information to myself and not tell any of the brigade. The most easily spotted inspector – the single man with no booze budget and an all-purpose respectable suit – tends to regularly get a fairly bizarre offering rather than a gastronomic tour de force. Enthusiastic kitchen crew will decorate the grub with knotted chives, twirls of fruit purée or towers of multicoloured vegetables. He will get twice the portion and twice the attention but he won't get food that is twice as good. At that point it is too late to change the quality of the raw material, the menu choice or the kitchen's skill.

Our menu shows the reality of cooking. It's a reflection of confidence that we don't use wow-presentation. I can make spun-sugar baskets, but choose not to. Chefs need to know where to stop and, if you know yourself the food is okay, at least there is one happy person.

SOUTHERN FRIED CHICKEN

Colonel Sander's lucrative chicken recipe didn't just pave the way for unsightly litter on street corners worldwide, it showed a style of cooking poultry which is popular and accessible. Yet, like fish and chips, this dish is rarely made properly, even at home.

FOR 4 PERSONS

2 boneless chicken breasts
2 boneless chicken thighs
1 tablespoon Dijon mustard
1 teaspoon milled black
*   pepper*
1 teaspoon salt
a pinch of cayenne pepper
150ml (5floz/scant 2/3 cup)
*   buttermilk*
4 rashers bacon
150g (5oz/2 1/2 cups) fresh
*   white breadcrumbs*
sunflower oil, for frying

Slice each breast and thigh into 4 pieces. Mix the mustard and seasonings together and brush them over the chicken pieces. Place the chicken in a bowl, pour over the buttermilk and turn the chicken pieces to ensure they are evenly coated.

Heat the oil in a wok or large frying pan to a depth of 1cm (1/2in). Fry the bacon until crisp. Lift out the rashers and, as soon as they are cool enough to handle, crumble them into small pieces and mix with the breadcrumbs.

Heat some more oil in the pan. Coat the chicken pieces with the breadcrumb mixture and fry for 7 to 10 minutes in the hot oil until golden brown.

POINTS TO WATCH

Temperature is crucial in this dish. If the oil is too hot, the coating will crisp up before the middle of the chicken is cooked. Be prepared to add more oil to the pan if it starts to smoke: this will lower the temperature.

FRESH PASTA WITH CHICKEN LIVERS, LEMON AND GARLIC

This sauce is creamy in appearance but contains little cream. The predominant flavour is from the olive oil which forms about one-third of its volume. Warmed olive oil would normally separate from the pasta and slide into a puddle at the bottom of the plate, but the texture created here by blending the oil with stock and cheese overcomes this. So why not use cream to achieve a creamy sauce? It seems reasonable, but unfortunately when used alone as the base of a sauce, cream is cloying and heavy, too much for something as mild as pasta.

FOR 4 PERSONS

1 batch of pasta (page 88)
500g (1lb 2oz) fresh chicken livers, trimmed
25g (1oz/¼ cup) grated Parmesan cheese
1 tablespoon chopped chives
FOR THE SAUCE
200ml (7floz/scant 1 cup) chicken stock
1 large clove garlic, chopped
50g (2oz/½ cup) grated Parmesan cheese
1 tablespoon crème fraîche
150ml (5floz/10 tablespoons) olive oil, plus extra for frying
1 tablespoon lemon juice
salt and pepper

Make and cook the pasta according to the recipe on page 88.

To make the sauce, heat the stock and garlic in a saucepan, then add the Parmesan and crème fraîche. Pour into a blender and process, adding the olive oil and lemon juice as it blends. Season to taste with salt and pepper.

Fry the chicken livers in a little oil until pink, then toss with the pasta and sauce. Garnish with Parmesan and chopped chives.

POINTS TO WATCH

This type of sauce is not as stable as one based on demi-glace or cream. If it is kept warm for a long time it will tend to separate but is easily returned to top condition by a short burst in the blender.

The thickness of the sauce will depend on the ratio of oil to stock. You can make it thicker if you prefer by increasing the proportion of oil, and make it thinner by lessening it.

STEAMED AND CRISP-FRIED DUCK WITH SPICED WINTER VEGETABLES

Duck production in Britain centred on the Buckinghamshire town of Aylesbury, after which the best known breed is named, although most duck we see in the shops come now from Norfolk and Lincolnshire. The Aylesbury duck is descended from the Chinese Pekin duck, a strain that has been bred for the table for around 2000 years. It is rich and fatty with a small amount of moist, tender flesh and a thick skin that turns sweet and crisp when cooked. To my mind this superb duck is the best type available, however it is not the only one on offer. Some varieties, like the French Barbary duck, need to be tackled in a completely different way, more like mallard or even steak. Ditto new British breeds like Gressingham or Lunesdale which are closer to the wild species.

FOR 4 PERSONS

2 x 2.5kg (5lb10oz) ducks
400g (14oz/2¾ cups)
    carrots
400g (14oz/2¾ cups)
    celeriac (celery root)
400g (14oz/2¾ cups)
    parsnip
400g (14oz/2¾ cups)
    swede (rutabaga)
2 tablespoons olive oil
1 tablespoon paprika
1 teaspoon ground
    cinnamon
1 teaspoon ground coriander
1 teaspoon ground cumin
1 teaspoon lemon juice
sunflower oil, for frying
salt and pepper

Steam the whole ducks for 1½ hours. Meanwhile, peel the root vegetables and cut them into 2cm (¾in) dice.

Fry the vegetables in the olive oil until they colour. Add the spices and stir for a few moments. Add enough water to cover, then boil until the vegetables are cooked and the liquid has evaporated. Add the lemon juice and season with salt and pepper.

When the ducks have finished steaming, remove the legs and take the breasts off the bone. If they cool down, then put the duck pieces back in the steamer for a few minutes.

Heat a frying pan with sunflower oil to a depth of 1cm (½in). Fry the duck pieces one at a time, on the skin side only. When crisp, lay them on mounds of the spiced root vegetables.

POINTS TO WATCH

Aylesbury duck has to be cooked well-done. There is a thickish membrane between the fat and meat that has to be melted away during cooking or it will be chewy.

If you do not have a pot big enough to steam both ducks at once, steam them one at a time.

Take care when frying the steamed duck as it will be wet and the moisture will make the hot oil splutter, which can cause burns. This is the moment for kitchen gloves and sleeves rolled right down.

The skin on the steamed duck will be fragile, so try to lift the duck out from underneath the backbone and use two spatulas to distribute the weight evenly.

WILD DUCK WITH CELERIAC AND MORELS

Wild duck is a dark, rich and distinctively flavoured meat. Provided it is served rare, it will be tender without the need for oil or butter. This recipe calls for mallard but the wild duck family also includes wigeon, which is smaller, and teal, which is smaller still. They all taste similar.

FOR 4 PERSONS

8 dried morel mushrooms
4 mallards
sunflower oil, for frying
2 shallots
1 small stick celery
2 cloves garlic
*100ml (3 1/2 floz/7 table-
    spoons) chicken stock or
    water*
50ml (2floz/1/4 cup) red wine
*1 small celeriac (celery root),
    peeled and diced*
*1 teaspoon grated
    horseradish*
*1 tablespoon double
    (heavy) cream*
*2 tablespoons demi-glace
    (page 30), optional*

In a small pan of water, bring the morels to the boil, then remove from the heat and set aside. When the morels are cool enough to handle, rinse, then cut off the stalks.

Cut the legs from the ducks. Fry these in a heavy pot along with the shallots, celery and garlic. Add the stock and red wine and bring to the boil. Cover and braise for 2 hours or until the meat is completely tender and ready to fall off the bone.

Heat a dry frying pan, then seal off the skin on each side of the ducks until dark. Transfer to a roasting tin and roast at 200°C (400°F/Gas 6) for about 25 minutes or until medium rare.

Peel and dice the celeriac. Boil it in some water until tender, then drain and mash it. Season with the horseradish, salt and pepper, stir in the cream and set aside.

Lift the braised legs from the pot and strain the cooking liquor into a small saucepan. Add the morels and stir until they come to the boil. Add the demi-glace if using.

Carve the duck breasts from the bone. Let them rest for a few minutes then slice fairly thinly. On warm serving plates, lay the braised leg against the celeriac purée and fan out the breast meat slices below. Pour the sauce around and serve.

POINTS TO WATCH

As with most birds, the legs have evolved for reasons other than culinary convenience and do not cook anywhere near as fast as the breast meat. This recipe braises them separately and the cooking liquor from this will form a major part of the accompanying sauce.

The skin on wild duck is leathery. Its only useful function is to protect the breast meat during cooking and it can be left on or dumped as you prefer.

The duck needs to be fried until the surface is dark in colour. The membrane between the skin and meat needs to have a lot of heat applied in order to melt away.

The carving method for any meat varies according to its texture. Tougher meats need to be carved much more thinly than tender ones, just as you would expect Parma ham to be sliced more thinly than boiled York ham. However, the thinner you slice, the swifter the meat will cool, so try to do this at the very last moment.

GRILLED MARINATED GUINEA FOWL

Guinea fowl meat is a touch gamier than chicken and not dissimilar to pheasant. When young, they suit being roasted, or grilled or broiled as here. Older specimens should be braised and will be dry to the point of toughness if you attempt any other treatment.

FOR 4 PERSONS

2 x 1kg (2lb 4oz) young guinea fowl

FOR THE MARINADE

100ml (3 1/2floz/7 table-spoons) olive oil

1 tablespoon lemon juice

1 tablespoon coriander seeds, lightly crushed

1 tablespoon marjoram or oregano

salt and pepper

Divide the guinea fowl into breasts and legs. Pull the legs away and downward from the breast so that they are horizontal with the work surface. The thigh bones will snap loose from their sockets and can then be cut off. Lift the flap of skin covering the narrow neck cavity and cut out the wishbone which frames this gap. Run your finger along the breastbone that divides the two breast fillets. Cut straight along each side of the bone until the breasts are completely free.

Mix the marinade ingredients together. Flatten each breast fillet with a small cutlet bat or the side of a heavy knife. Toss the breasts, and legs if you are using them, in the marinade and leave in the refrigerator for 3 hours.

Grill or broil the guinea fowl, which should take 20 minutes for the breasts and 40 minutes for the legs. Baste with any leftover marinade and serve with green salad.

POINTS TO WATCH

Marinating affects flavour and texture. The more powerful the marinade, the less any fine nuances of quality in the bird will matter. The purpose here is to tenderize and moisten the meat, not to overpower it, so a brief spell in the herb and oil mixture is all that's needed.

The legs take much longer to cook than the breast meat and are really better braised.

When portioning the guinea fowl, cut downwards keeping the blade next to the bone. Do not leave the fingers of your left hand (if you're right-handed) under the part you are boning in case the knife slips.

You don't want the fillet to be thin, just even in thickness from top to bottom. The whacking also helps to tenderize the meat.

ROAST PARTRIDGE WITH HARICOT BEANS AND SMOKED BACON

There are two types of partridge, red legged or French partridge, and grey or English partridge. They are both raised and shot in England so there is little point in anyone choosing the latter specifically for patriotic reasons. However, the grey are held to be finer and cost more. Only the young birds should be roasted as the meat has a tendency to be dry. In Britain, game birds are generally wild creatures and even those reared by gamekeepers, like partridge, will usually be bred for their hunting qualities, not for any succulence on the dining table.

FOR 4 PERSONS

4 partridges
olive oil, for brushing
25g (1oz/1/4 stick) butter
100g (31/2oz) smoked
* streaky bacon, in one piece*
2 shallots
2 medium carrots
400ml (14floz/13/4 cups)
* chicken stock*
8 waxy potatoes, such as
* Charlotte or Yukon Gold,*
* scrubbed*
25g (1oz/2 tablespoons)
* cooked haricot beans*
25g (1oz) chorizo sausage
100g (31/2oz/3/4 cup) savoy
* cabbage, shredded*
2 tablespoons demi-glace
* (page 30)*

Heat the oven to 200°C (400°F/Gas 6). Coat the birds with olive oil and fry on each side in a hot, dry pan until the legs start to brown. Lift the partridges onto a roasting tray and coat with lots of soft butter, then roast them for 20 minutes.

Meanwhile, dice the piece of bacon and chop the shallots. Cut the carrots into 2cm (3/4in) pieces. Heat a large heavy casserole and fry the bacon, shallots and carrots. Add the stock, potatoes and haricot beans and bring to the boil.

When the potatoes are almost cooked, add the chorizo and roast partridge. Cover and cook in the oven for 20 minutes, adding the cabbage to the casserole after 15 minutes.

To serve, lay the partridge on top of the vegetables and bacon on warm plates. Add the demi-glace to the cooking liquor remaining in the casserole and boil to reduce the mixture to a sauce consistency. Pour the sauce around the plates and serve.

POINTS TO WATCH

You need lots of butter or oil to compensate for the lack of fat in the meat. Using olive oil rather than other vegetable oils will allow the birds to colour faster.

Autumn and winter are the prime time for game birds in Britain – partridge starts in September and ends in February. Don't forget that there is an end to each bird's season and that the quality of the older birds may well be different towards the end of the season.

Meat cookery

There is a lot of nonsense talked about well-done meat. In fact, the longer meat is cooked, the more its flavour develops – but at a real loss to texture. It's a question of making the best use of your ingredient and it isn't any form of 'food fascism' to realise that a fatless piece of meat grilled until well-done is as daft as an under-done stew. A thick piece of fillet steak cooked well-done is a waste of money because the cut does not suit the purpose, but a thin steak cooked well-done will have proportionately more caramelized surface to inside meat,

It's a question of making the best use of your ingredient.

so is less at risk of ending up dull and dry. It isn't my preference to roast meat well-done either, but at least the juices that escape during protracted cooking provide wonderful gravy.

For those who don't like to see blood in their red meat, braising is a better option. Long cooking suits gelatinous joints wonderfully and many of the world's great meat dishes are braised or stewed – think of cassoulet, osso bucco or boeuf bourguignon. The method involves browning the surface of the meat before adding liquid such as stock, wine or water to finish the cooking process slowly. Methods such as this and boiling (a misnomer, for you only want a slight simmer when cooking meat) are usually, but not exclusively, employed for cheaper, tougher joints and these can demand more skill than their expensive counterparts on the butcher's slab. They also require good judgement with herbs and spices.

Assessing meat's doneness becomes easier with experience but is essential to learn quickly if you are cooking for other people in return for money. In an emergency you can always cook meat a little more, though once sliced, it tends to turn grey. Only magic will make the meat less cooked if it has been in the pan too long. Large joints need to be pierced with a skewer for real information but, for a steak or chop, this is what you do:

Press the meat with your index finger. If it feels like there is a hard rubber ball inside, then the meat is still blue. The more it cooks from this stage, the more it will give to your touch. However, from the point where it is becoming medium to well-done, the meat will start to harden and this firmness has a completely different feel to the hardness of the first stage when the meat was very underdone. Residual heat will continue to cook the meat while it is resting and, in fact, right up to the time when it is eaten or goes cold. Give yourself a little leeway and, if in doubt, cut the meat in half and look. In these cases you can serve it with a nouvelle cuisine presentation – your guest will find you bizarrely old-fashioned but at least you will know the damned thing is cooked. In time, after a lot of steaks, it will be second nature.

BOEUF À LA FICELLE

Ficelle is French for string and in this case the string does not come as flavouring or even garnish. The dish's title indicates the cooking method, for the steaks are suspended in simmering stock by means of a piece of string. It is closely related to pot au feu and bollito misto, where the meat is poached rather than grilled, broiled or fried, but with one major difference: instead of long, slow cooking of gelatinous joints, the dish calls for a prime cut – fillet steak or short loin. The result should be rare or medium-rare, like any other good steak preparation.

FOR 4 PERSONS

1 litre (1 3/4 pints/4 1/2 cups) veal stock
a few new potatoes
a few carrots
a stick of celery
a few leeks
4 beef fillet steaks (short loin), 200g (7oz) each
FOR THE RELISH
1 tablespoon grated horseradish
1 tablespoon wholegrain mustard
1 teaspoon lemon juice
1 tablespoon double (heavy) cream
salt and pepper

Bring the stock to the boil. Meanwhile, peel and scrape the vegetables. Drop the potatoes into the boiling stock; the remaining vegetables may be bundled in string for cooking or dropped in loose as with the potatoes. Do not add salt.

Add the remaining vegetables in the order in which they take to cook: carrots first, then celery, and finally leeks. Around the same time as you add the celery, tie some kitchen string round each piece of steak and drop them into the simmering stock.

Mix together a relish: I use a mixture of grated horseradish, wholegrain mustard, lemon juice and a little cream. Any mustard, or creamed horseradish, will do just as well.

Lift out the steaks. If you are unsure how cooked they are, cut them in half and look. You can always put them back in the stock for a few minutes. Lift out the vegetables too and arrange both meat and vegetables in large bowls or deep plates.

Pour over some stock and serve with the relish. As with pot au feu, the cooking liquor is drunk first and the meat and vegetables are eaten afterwards: two courses in one dish.

POINTS TO WATCH

The cooking time for the meat will be similar to conventional grilling or broiling. Although the temperature of the stock will never rise above boiling point (much lower than the temperature reached in a frying pan), the meat is being cooked from all sides simultaneously and this will compensate.

It is never a good idea to literally boil meat. Simmering at, or just below, boiling point is what is needed. A rolling boil affects texture, giving a drier, less juicy result.

The meat and vegetables need to be covered with stock and the more liquid there is in the pot, the less the temperature will be reduced when the meat drops in, so it cooks more evenly and quickly.

The idea is that everything should finish cooking simultaneously, so be sure to add the vegetables in the order in which they take to cook.

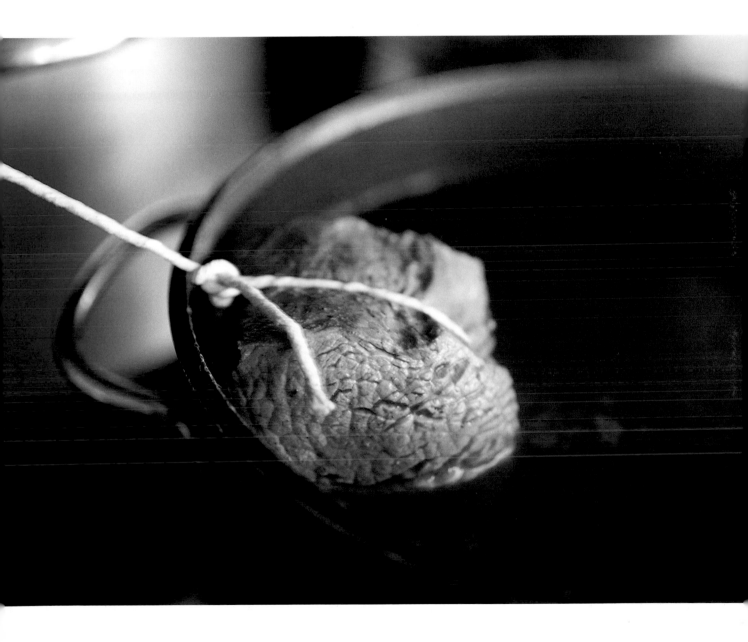

ROAST LOIN OF VEAL WITH MARSALA

The combination of veal and marsala wine, as in piccata alla marsala, was an Italian restaurant staple in the 1960s and when the tired trattoria repertoire of pollo cacciatore and mediocre spaghetti dishes slid into oblivion, the dish suffered an unworthy decline.

Loin of veal roasted rather than batted out for escalopes has two advantages. The quality of the meat comes to the fore and the roasting process gives a lift to the sauce by providing wonderful cooking juices. It has disadvantages, too, of course. The traditional business of flattening the veal would tenderize the meat and mean that lesser, cheaper, cuts could be used. Also, a lot less meat is needed.

FOR 4 PERSONS

4 veal fillets cut from the loin, 200g (7oz) each

4 teaspoons olive oil

1 stick celery, cut into 3cm (1 1/4in) lengths

2 shallots, peeled and quartered

4 tablespoons marsala wine

100ml (3 1/2floz/scant 1/2 cup) demi-glace (page 30)

25g (1oz/1/4 stick) unsalted butter

a few drops of lemon juice, optional

salt and pepper

Heat the oven to 200°C (400°F/Gas 6). Meanwhile, on the stovetop, heat a frying pan.

Season the veal with salt and pepper, then brush with olive oil. Sear the meat quickly on all sides and remove from the pan. Add the celery and shallot to the pan and fry until browned.

Transfer the meat and vegetables to a roasting tray and cook in the oven until medium rare, around 20 minutes. Let the cooked veal rest in the tray for 5 minutes, then lift it out for carving.

Deglaze the roasting tray with the marsala and sieve the mixture into a small saucepan. Add the demi-glace and bring to the boil. Whisk in the unsalted butter. Check the seasoning of the sauce: if it is too sweet, add a few drops of lemon juice to bring it into balance. Serve hot with the roast veal.

POINTS TO WATCH

I hate to join the nationalistic band but British veal, if you can find it, is vastly superior to either the Dutch or even French, both of which sacrifice flavour for whiteness of flesh. There are no ethical problems with it either.

The meat may be cooked on the bone just like the venison saddle (page 148). But veal bones make the very best stock, so I always remove them and roast them separately to make demi-glace. The flesh I cook in steak-sized fillets.

In the pan, veal tends to lose moisture fast, bubbling and braising rather than frying or roasting, so swift searing helps keep its flavour intense.

If you have no veal stock or demi-glace, this dish is still possible. The veal's cooking liquor may be heated with a little extra marsala, then thickened by adding butter. It will be lighter in colour but otherwise fine.

Marsala need not be cloyingly sweet. I use Terre Arse marsala which has sweet notes but also the balance of an oloroso sherry.

RACK OF LAMB WITH GARLIC

Meat cooked on the bone is better than meat cooked in fillets. The bones stretch the meat so that it doesn't shrivel in the heat and the little bits of fat surrounding the bone help to baste and moisten the meat as it cooks. However, I generally carve cooked meat from the bone before serving so that the plate contains only what is meant to be eaten and not some graveyard of animal skeletons. The one exception is rack of lamb, for the nuggets of meat along and between the bones are among the sweetest and tastiest you can find.

FOR 4 PERSONS

24 cloves wet or new
  season garlic
4 racks of lamb
a little olive oil, for frying and
  brushing
1 shallot, peeled and
  quartered
100ml (3 1/2floz/scant
  1/2 cup) chicken stock
salt

FOR THE BASTE

4 tablespoons olive oil
2 tablespoons chopped
  parsley
6 basil leaves
1 teaspoon finely grated
  lemon zest
1 teaspoon freshly ground
  black pepper, plus extra
  for seasoning

Boil the cloves of garlic in a pan of water until they are soft.

Meanwhile, trim the membrane and fat from the racks of lamb – you should be left with bare meat and bones with only a fine coating of fat. Fry the trimmings with the shallot until brown, then deglaze the pan with the stock to make a good gravy base. Transfer the liquid to a jug or bowl and clean out the frying pan.

To make the baste, blend the olive oil, parsley, basil, lemon zest and pepper in a blender.

Heat the oven to 200°C (400°F/Gas 6) and, on the stovetop, reheat the frying pan. Season the racks with salt and pepper and brush with olive oil. Sear the racks quickly on each side in the hot pan, then put them and the poached garlic in a roasting tray. Roast for 20 minutes for pink, longer for well-done.

Lift the meat from the roasting tray and deglaze the tray with the gravy stock made earlier. Bring to the boil and let this sauce reduce a little. Meanwhile, paint the herb and oil baste over the racks. Sieve the sauce over the racks of lamb and serve.

POINTS TO WATCH

There is a rubbery membrane between the eye of the meat and the fat just underneath the skin. This needs to be cut away if the meat is to be served pink (it will melt by the time the meat is well-done). To do this, lift up the flap of skin and back fat and cut it off completely.

A rack of lamb is still a novel cut of meat to some butchers, for whom it represents one side of the joint known as a best end of lamb. Make sure that the butcher chops the racks competely away from the central chine bone and that none of this is left attached, for it makes carving awkward once served.

Olive oil is best for brushing onto small joints like this, or for steaks that are to be grilled, but not because of the oil's flavour, so this isn't the moment for your estate bottled, extra virgin, cold pressed stuff. Olive oil has a low flash point so the meat will colour better and faster than if brushed with any other oil.

Water plus 2 tablespoons of demi-glace (page 30) can be used in place of the chicken stock, if necessary.

MIDDLE EASTERN DRY MARINATED RACK OF LAMB

You can extend the Middle Eastern theme of this dish by serving it with rice or flat bread. However, in the Lebanon I've found that they do eat plenty of potato – both as a mezze and with meat, so I guess everything is authentic if you want it to be.

FOR 4 PERSONS

4 racks of lamb

1 small or 1/2 large red bell pepper

1 small red chilli, deseeded

2 cloves garlic

1 tablespoon chopped mint

1 teaspoon ground coriander

1 tablespoon ground cumin

1 teaspoon saffron threads

2 tablespoons olive oil

salt and black pepper

Trim away most of the fat and all of the membrane covering the eye of the meat. Season with salt and pepper.

Chop the bell pepper, chilli, garlic, mint and spices together until the mixture is almost a pulp. Stir in the olive oil, then rub this mixture into the meat. Wrap the coated racks in plastic wrap and place in the refrigerator for 2-3 hours.

Heat the oven to 200°C (400°F/Gas 6). Heat a dry frying pan then, working one at a time, add the racks and cook until sealed on the outside.

Transfer the racks to a roasting tray and roast until pink – around 10 minutes. Leave the racks in the tray to rest for a few minutes before serving. The pan juices will make an excellent sauce when simply poured over the meat.

POINTS TO WATCH

The longer the lamb marinates, the more pronounced the flavour change: 2-3 hours suits my palate for I like to taste the lamb as well as the spices.

Preparing a loin of pork

A loin of pork from a traditional breed will have far more fat than you are accustomed to seeing on regular farmed pork. The fat will be sweet and delicious, but still may be a little too much for some people. Cutting it away means losing the crackling, so the choice is yours.

Use a boning knife to cut the loin free of the rib bones. This is easily accomplished (providing the butcher has removed the chine or backbone) by following the line of bones downwards with a sharp knife. Keep the blade right next to and always pointing towards the bone and you will not lose valuable meat, or valuable fingers, should the knife slip. The bones you cut away will be excellent for spare rib dishes another time.

Slice off as much fat as you feel necessary. Lift up the remaining white fat to expose the rubbery membrane that runs the length of the loin right next to the meat. Take a sharp knife and slice this off, then replace the white fat to baste the meat while it cooks.

ROAST PORK LOIN WITH BRAISED TROTTER

Loin of pork can be dry. Old breeds, such as Berkshire, Tamworth and Gloucestershire Old Spot, reared outdoors and properly fed, have vastly superior meat but also a tendency to be overly fat. I love this sweet back fat but am happy to trim it ruthlessly for those who do not (see previous page).

Pig's trotters cost almost nothing. They were temporarily in vogue a decade back when chefs took to filleting them and shovelling super-expensive titbits like morel mushrooms and calves' sweetbreads inside. I read somewhere that this is as easy as removing a kid glove but have found in practice that it is a time-consuming nuisance. You may add sweetbreads and morels to the mixture here should you want, but what's essential to the dish is that you have the deeply savoury taste of the braised trotters in an easily tackled form to contrast with the roast loin.

Mashed parsnip or potato works well with the finished dish and the cooking juices from both the roasting tray and braising pan combine nicely to make a good gravy.

FOR 4 PERSONS

4 pig's trotters
a little oil, for frying
1 carrot, roughly chopped
1 medium onion, roughly chopped
500ml (18floz/2 1/4 cups) stock or water
1 tablespoon chopped parsley
800g/1lb 12oz pork loin, well-trimmed
1 tablespoon demi-glace (page 30), optional
salt and pepper

Heat the oven to 170°C (325°F/Gas 3). Split the pig's trotters lengthways and season with salt and pepper. Fry them in a casserole dish until coloured. Add the carrot and onion, then pour on enough stock or water to cover. Cover with the lid and transfer to the oven to cook for 2 hours, or until the meat has come away from the bones and is quite soft.

Drain the cooking liquor from the trotters into a bowl and pick out any bones you can find. Chop the flesh (do not use a food processor) and moisten it with the cooking liquor. Keep this mixture warm in a saucepan, adding the chopped parsley and, if needed, some more salt and pepper.

Roast the loin for about 35-40 minutes at 200°C (400°F/Gas 6), then leave it on a plate to rest while you make the gravy.

Add any remaining trotter stock to the roasting tray and boil to deglaze the pan. Sieve the mixture into a saucepan and simmer for a few moments to reduce – if you have any demi-glace sauce base, you can add a tablespoon of it also.

Spoon the trotter mixture onto each plate and lay slices of roast loin alongside. Serve with the gravy.

POINTS TO WATCH

Salt the trotters and leave them to soak in water overnight before cooking.

Pork is best cooked through. If you like it very well-done, leave a little more fat on the joint so that it does not dry out too much in the oven.

The thickness of the pork loin is one of several factors determining the exact cooking time. I use Berkshire pork, off the bone, and find that a piece for 4 people takes 35-40 minutes at 200°C (400°F/Gas 6). The important thing is that it is cooked all the way through.

A pastry cutter used as a mould will help you make a tidy job of placing the trotter mixture on the serving plate.

CALVES' SWEETBREADS WITH WARM DRESSING AND POTATO AND OLIVE CAKES

Sweetbreads are sold as either heartbreads or throatbreads. The better of the two are the fist-shaped heartbreads. These are thymus glands and, despite all the male sniggering whenever they appear on the menu, have no connection whatsoever with delicacies from the trouser area. They are expensive and have become a luxury item. A small portion, though, makes a fine first course, providing that the accompanying potato and olive cake is also smaller than usual. If you have veal demi-glace, a warmed teaspoonful served over the sweetbreads is especially fine.

FOR 4 PERSONS

*750g (1lb 10oz) calves'
    sweetbreads*
a dash of vinegar
a little olive oil, for frying
*4 potato and olive cakes
    (page 78)*
salt and pepper
FOR THE DRESSING
1 tablespoon Dijon mustard
*1 tablespoon white wine
    vinegar*
1 egg yolk
*100ml (3 1/2floz/scant
    1/2 cup) sunflower oil*
*100ml (3 1/2floz/scant
    1/2 cup) olive oil*
*100ml (3 1/2floz/scant
    1/2 cup) veal stock or
    water*
1 tablespoon capers
*1 tablespoon chopped
    shallot*
*1 tablespoon chopped
    parsley*

Soak the sweetbreads for at least 1 hour in cold water. Cut away most of the membrane from the outside, leaving just enough to hold the sweetbreads together.

Place the sweetbreads in a saucepan with a dash of vinegar, a little salt and pepper and enough water to just cover. Top with a circle of greaseproof or parchment paper, or the wrapping from a pack of butter. Bring to the boil, simmer for 3 minutes, then remove from the heat and leave to cool in the cooking liquor. The sweetbreads should look set but still be soft to the touch.

Take out the sweetbreads and cut them into even, rather thick slices. Season and brush with olive oil, then fry them in a hot pan until brown on each side. If the slices are very thick or the sweetbreads were particularly soft, they will need a further 5 minutes in a hot oven while you prepare the dressing and cook the potato and olive cakes.

Make the dressing by mixing together the mustard, vinegar and egg yolk in a bowl. Gradually whisk in the oils – like mayonnaise.

In a small saucepan, heat the stock or water with the capers, shallot and parsley. Bring to the boil, then remove the saucepan from the direct heat and whisk in the dressing. You can keep the mixture warm but do not reboil.

Spoon the dressing onto warmed plates. Lay the sweetbreads on top and a potato cake to one side, then serve.

POINTS TO WATCH

The preparation of this dish has two distinct phases. The sweetbreads have to be blanched then allowed to cool in their cooking liquor so that they set firm but are still soft. This is best done an hour or so before you want to cook the rest of the dish.

The sauce here is a warm emulsion of veal stock and a mayonnaise-like mustard dressing. It is liable to separate if boiled.

VEAL KIDNEY WITH RED WINE AND CASSIS

Pale is good when it comes to veal kidneys. If they are too dark, soak them in a mixture of milk and water overnight. The preparation of this dish is as important as the cooking process, for if the mass of white fat and its rubbery connections to the meat are not painstakingly and meticulously removed, the kidneys will be an adventure to eat rather than a pleasure.

FOR 4 PERSONS

2 veal kidneys
1 tablespoon olive oil
50ml (2floz/1/4 cup) red wine
1 teaspoon crème de cassis
50g (2oz/1/2 stick) unsalted butter, cubed
1 tablespoon chopped chives
salt and pepper

Make a cut through the centre of the kidneys, dividing them into two equal pieces. Use the tip of a sharp knife to cut the fat and connective tissue from each kidney. Pull away the membrane that covers the outside of each one. This should leave you with pale and shiny meat. Season the kidneys with salt and pepper and brush with the olive oil.

Heat a pan and fry the kidneys quickly on both sides. They will soon produce quite a bit of liquid that will start to bubble. Remove the pan from the direct heat.

Pour the pan juices into a separate saucepan with the red wine and cassis and place over a low heat. Whisk in the butter and chives to make the sauce, then serve with the fried kidneys.

POINTS TO WATCH

Crème de cassis is a highly concentrated liqueur made from blackcurrants and is most commonly used to flavour white wine for a Kir. Just a drop will transform a glass of wine, so it's best to use a similar proportion for the sauce here. The idea is that you are adding a touch of sweetness as well as a hint of the fruit flavour.

The menu at The Merchant House is market-based. It reflects the best of what was available on any specific date. Buy good ingredients and you need to mutilate them in order to produce bad meals. Buy rubbish and you need more skill than most chefs possess to produce something worth getting fat for.

I type the menu, the results of the day's shopping and preparation, only minutes before the first person is due. There is no printed card dictating that asparagus should be on offer when artichokes are obviously in better condition, or that venison has to be on the menu when there are first-rate hares to be had.

There is a street market in Ludlow three days a week (four in summer) and this helps with supply, but in Britain there is not the same culture of buying at street markets that there is in countries such as France. If you see someone in a chef's uniform early in the morning wandering round the stalls, you can be sure there is a photographer not far behind taking pictures for a glossy magazine or book.

In fact, most restaurant shopping is done on the phone. Dealers call and let you know what is coming in and, if pressed, how much it costs. Despite this, I think there is an advantage to walking round as many shops and stalls as practicable, to see and touch the produce before coming to a menu decision. Each morning I tour Ludlow's food shops to poke at the raspberries and rhubarb, eat slivers of cheese at the town's excellent cheese shop, and assess what is at its best and what is coming to an end. There's no denying it makes a pleasant change, for an hour, from the small, hot kitchen, especially on a warm summer day.

SADDLE OF VENISON

If you have bought well-hung, well-flavoured venison, the last thing to consider is masking its taste and texture with a marinade or inflicting some pointless massage of spices onto its surface. Well-hung meat will have a developed a distinctive taste and the traditional course has been to counter any rankness or gamey flavour with something sweet, the same logic that paired mutton with redcurrant jelly. Most venison is not gamey enough to need this and, just as the logic of mutton and redcurrant jam is ludicrous when used for delicate new season lamb, the sweetness of heavy port and fruit-based sauces is irrelevant to the venison now available. I like to match its texture with that of goats' cheese gnocchi (page 82) or to make a soft mash of potato and then add a few wild mushrooms to the cooking juices.

FOR 4 PERSONS

10g (1/2oz/1/2 cup) dried
  morel mushrooms
2kg (4lb 8oz) saddle of
  venison
1 medium carrot, roughly
  chopped
1 stick celery, roughly
  chopped
1 medium onion, peeled
  and quartered
50ml (2floz/1/4 cup)
  red wine
1 teaspoon arrowroot
25g (1oz/1/4 stick) unsalted
  butter
salt and pepper

In a small pan of water, bring the morels to the boil, then remove from the heat and set aside. When the morels are cool enough to handle, rinse, then cut off the stalks and slice in half.

Heat the oven to 200°C (400°F/Gas 6). Trim away everything extraneous from the saddle of venison and leave only the meat and bones. Cut up these trimmings and place in a roasting tray to cook alongside the saddle and help to flavour the sauce.

Carefully cut away the membrane that covers the eye of the meat and brush the exposed fillet with olive oil. Season with salt and pepper, then place in the roasting tray. Add the carrot, celery and onion and roast until medium-rare. The meat will probably take 30 to 40 minutes depending on thickness.

Let the joint rest for 3 to 4 minutes in the roasting tray so that any meat juices may run back into the sauce base. Lift the saddle of venison out for carving.

Pour the red wine and 200ml (7floz/scant 1 cup) of water into the roasting tray and deglaze it. Bring the mixture to the boil, then strain into a small saucepan.

Add the morels and return the sauce to the boil. In a small bowl, mix the arrowroot with 1 teaspoon of water and add to the pan. Bring the sauce back to the boil and whisk in the butter to finish. Serve with the carved meat.

POINTS TO WATCH
There can be grit inside the dried mushrooms so rinse them well after reconstitution.

Turn the meat over halfway through cooking so that it cooks evenly and does not become dry on the side nearest the roasting tray.

ROAST SADDLE AND JUGGED LEG OF HARE

Hare is generally cooked long and slow. The word jugged indicates that the blood of the animal was heated in a jug over hot water – a bain-marie in kitchen terminology – until it thickened, and then was used to enrich the cooking liquor. I don't like the flavour this creates, so pass on this aspect of traditional cookery. The saddle is roasted rare and, as with the roast and braised wild duck dish on page 128, contrasts nicely in subtlety and texture with the slow-cooked legs.

FOR 4 PERSONS

2 young hares
a little sunflower oil, for
  frying
500ml (18floz/2 1/4 cups)
  chicken stock
1 tablespoon plain
  (all-purpose) flour
a little grated nutmeg
1 onion, chopped
1 stick celery, chopped
1 medium carrot, chopped
150ml (5floz/2/3 cup)
  red wine
1 tablespoon potato flour
  (fécule)
salt and freshly ground black
  pepper

Joint the hare. You will need to remove first the back legs by pulling them back from their sockets and cutting them away with a sharp knife. Similarly, remove the front shoulders and, finally, trim the remaining saddle of its flaps of skin.

Fry the front shoulders and any trimmings in a little oil, then place in a large pan with the chicken stock and cook for 1 hour to give a game stock. Top up with water if it reduces too much.

Dust the hare legs with flour and season with nutmeg, salt and pepper. Brown them in a hot frying pan, then transfer to a heavy lidded pot or casserole.

Heat the oven to 180°C (350°F/Gas 4). Fry the onion, celery and carrot and put these in the pot with the hare legs. Pour on the game stock and red wine, then cover and cook in the oven for 2 1/2 hours or until the meat is completely tender.

Raise the oven temperature to 220°C (425°F/Gas 7). Brush the saddles with oil, season with salt and pepper and roast for 15 minutes. The meat cooks quickly and should be rare.

Strain the cooking liquor from the casserole into a saucepan and bring it to the boil, skimming the surface. Whisk the potato flour with 1 tablespoon of water and add to the sauce to thicken.

Carve the fillets from the saddle, slice them lengthways and lay alongside the braised legs. Serve with the sauce.

POINTS TO WATCH
The stock may smell a bit ripe as it cooks but do not lose heart for it will taste fine.

The liquid used to braise the hare legs is not just a cooking medium, it will also provide the sauce for the dish. If the level of liquid reduces too much during cooking, top it up with extra water so that there is enough to give a good sauce for serving.

Desserts and pastries

Dessert should provide a complete change of pace, style and maybe temperature to the rest of the meal. The table is cleared, the bread and seasonings removed – it is almost as though you are sitting at a different table. Nobody is hungry, so whatever is on offer must tempt for reasons other than appetite. At The Merchant House we find that, however filling the preceeding dishes, most customers are determined to have a pudding. At dinner parties too, guests tend to be disappointed if there is no dessert and it can seem as though the meal was cut short without the full three courses.

However, mid-meal sorbets are a bad idea. Anyone who has been treated to this at a wedding banquet or somesuch will know it is one of the grimmer aspects of grandiose dining, leaving guests

Mid-meal sorbets are a bad idea.

with a mouthful of sugar syrup before the savoury main course is tackled. The renowned French gastronome and guidebook editor Henri Gault said that, once given a sorbet, he always asked for his hat and coat as the meal had obviously finished. This would be excessive behaviour at a family occasion; you will find a look of patronising disdain is quite sufficient.

Most desserts revolve around fruit, custard or pastry, with chocolate and nuts helping things along, especially through the winter months when fruit is scarce. The permutations are endless and the well-established combinations such as peaches with raspberries, or cinnamon with apple, can be deconstructed, then reworked into different dishes with one flavour perhaps being used for ice cream and another made into tart or soufflé. This gives plenty of scope to those cooks who want to innovate without actually departing from good taste and balance in the process.

Attention to the seasons is a help when compiling menus. Whether it is purely a matter of association or something much deeper, soft fruit like raspberries, cherries and peaches seem perfect for warm sunny days, while apples or pears with maybe butterscotch and toasted nuts seem right in late autumn. Seasonal fruit is in any case fresher and cheaper at the appropriate time of year.

Pastry making is probably the trickiest part of a dessert course but becomes easier with practice. It is the one area of kitchen work where a strict adherence to the ratios in a recipe is important – and one reason why otherwise casually confident chefs, used to making sauces and fish fillets do whatever they want, often keep well clear of the pastry section. In fact, well-made pastry, from top quality ingredients like unsalted butter, will differentiate your dish from run-of-the-mill or commercially made items far more effectively than any quirky embellishment read about in a glossy magazine or cookbook. Master a couple of good pastry recipes and there are thousands of tarts and pies that can easily be put together to suit the season and the shopping.

Making puff pastry

Mix together all the ingredients except the chilled butter to make a dough. Then roll the dough out to a cross shape (St George rather than St Andrew) 0.5cm (1/4in) thick.

Between two sheets of plastic wrap, roll the block of chilled butter into a square so that it fits neatly into the centre of the pastry cross you have made. Fold over all the flaps of pastry to enclose the butter, creating a pastry parcel.

You will then need to complete four 'book turns' with an interval between each for the pastry to rest. A book turn is done this way: roll the pastry out into a long strip like a stair carpet, fold each end into the middle of the strip, then close the newly formed ends like a book. There will be four layers of pastry. Put the pastry to rest in the fridge and repeat the rolling, turning and resting process three times.

Do not use butter that is too cold and hard as it is difficult to roll. Similarly, take the pastry out of the refrigerator 10 minutes before performing each book turn so that it softens enough to roll without breaking the layers.

CARAMEL AND APPLE TART

This tart is a classic tarte fine aux pommes with the addition of a dark caramel sauce. It is not as sweet as my butterscotch tart (page 158) for the sugar in this recipe is burnt before any cream is added.

There is always a danger of becoming cocky with simple dishes such as this. I once made it as part of a demonstration to a large theatre with fellow chef Alastair Little. I didn't notice until too late that the oven, though brightly lit, had never been switched on. Alastair blustered while I grilled the tart so that it would at least look edible, but I'm sure we fooled nobody.

FOR 4 PERSONS

FOR THE PUFF PASTRY

450g (1lb/4 sticks) unsalted
   butter
500g (1lb 2oz) plain flour
   (4 cups unbleached
   pastry flour)
1½ teaspoons salt
25ml (1floz/1½ tablespoons)
   white wine vinegar

FOR THE APPLE TART

½ batch of puff pastry
   (above)
4 Cox's orange pippins
   or tart eating apples
25g (1oz/¼ stick) unsalted
   butter
1 tablespoon caster
   (granulated) sugar
a little icing (powdered)
   sugar, for dusting

FOR THE SAUCE

250g (9oz/1¼ cups)
   granulated sugar
175g (6oz/1½ sticks)
   unsalted butter
150ml (5floz/⅔ cup)
   double (heavy) cream

To make the pastry, place 400g (14oz/3½ sticks) of the butter in the fridge to chill thoroughly. Meanwhile, gently melt the remaining 50g (2oz/½ stick) in a small saucepan.

Place the flour and salt in a large bowl. Mix in the vinegar, melted butter and 200ml (7floz/¾ cup) of cold water to make a dough. Roll it out into a cross shape and incorporate the chilled butter as instructed on (page 152). You need only half the batch of puff pastry for this recipe.

To complete the apple tarts, roll out the finished pastry as thinly as possible into four flat discs and prick them all over with a fork.

Heat the oven to 200°C (400°F/Gas 6). Peel, core and slice the apples, then spread them across the top of the pastry discs. Dot with the butter and sprinkle with sugar.

Place the apple tarts on a baking sheet and cook in the oven until crisp – this will take 15 to 20 minutes.

To make the sauce, heat the sugar until it starts to caramelize, then stir in the butter. When the colour deepens to a nutty brown, let the mixture cool for a few seconds, then add the cream and bring to the boil.

Pour the caramel sauce around the hot apple tarts, dust with icing sugar and serve. A scoop of vanilla or cinnamon ice cream can be a welcome addition at this stage too.

POINTS TO WATCH

Once the discs of pastry have been rolled out and topped with apple slices, they can be kept in the freezer until needed, making this a very handy dish for dinner party hosts.

Take care as you add the cream to the caramel mixture as it will splutter. Always let caramel cool for a few seconds before adding any liquid.

RHUBARB TART WITH GINGER CUSTARD

Rhubarb and custard is a much-loved, time-tested partnership and, like most such combinations, is well received when reworked into other formats, such as a tart made with a basic sweet pastry. Only use tender forced rhubarb for this recipe, the summer outdoor variety is tough and coarse.

FOR 8 PERSONS

FOR THE SWEET PASTRY

2 medium (large) egg yolks

225g (8oz/2 sticks) unsalted
    butter

1 heaped tablespoon caster
    (granulated) sugar

275g (10oz) plain flour
    (2 1/4 cups unbleached
    all-purpose flour)

FOR THE FILLING

1kg (2lb 4oz) forced rhubarb

150g (5oz/1 cup) caster
    (granulated) sugar

2 medium (large) egg yolks

75ml (3floz/1/3 cup) double
    (heavy) cream

FOR THE CUSTARD

3 medium (large) egg yolks

50g (2oz/1/3 cup) caster
    (granulated) sugar

275ml (10floz/1 1/4 cups)
    milk

40g (1 1/2oz/2 tablespoons)
    crystallized ginger, chopped

To make the pastry, beat the egg yolks and butter together in a large bowl, then beat in the sugar. Stir in the flour and knead just once or twice to mix thoroughly.

Wrap the pastry in plastic wrap and rest in the fridge for at least 1 hour before use.

Heat the oven to 200°C (400°F/Gas 6). Line a 26cm (10in) flan case with the pastry and bake for 15 minutes. Leave the oven on when you remove the tart case.

To make the filling, cut the rhubarb into 3cm (1 1/4in) lengths. Cook it in a saucepan with 100g (3 1/2oz/2/3 cup) of the sugar for 4 minutes or until the rhubarb is cooked but still firm. Transfer the rhubarb to the baked pastry case.

Whisk the 2 egg yolks with the remaining 50g (1 1/2oz/1/3 cup) of sugar and the cream and pour this mixture over the rhubarb. Place in the oven to bake for 40 minutes.

Make the ginger custard by whisking together the egg yolks and sugar. In a saucepan, heat the milk and crystallized ginger to boiling point, then whisk into the egg mixture. Return the custard to the saucepan and cook gently until it starts to thicken – this will take about 10 minutes. Do not let it boil.

Cut a wedge of tart per person and serve the custard separately.

POINTS TO WATCH

The pastry calls for the butter and egg to be creamed together before the flour is added. This reduces the risk of over-handling the pastry but for success the butter needs to be cool rather than cold and hard.

Rest the pastry each time you handle it – to line the flan tin for instance – otherwise it will shrink as it cooks.

The pastry looks awkward to handle when rolled because of its high butter content. If you prefer, it can be rolled in pieces and fitted like a jigsaw into the tart case without problem.

BUTTERSCOTCH TART

I am not sure whether this is a traditional Lake District dish or whether it was the invention of the late Francis Coulson at Sharrow Bay in Ullswater. Probably a bit of both. The topping looks terribly rich but is in fact a mixture of whipped cream in equal proportion to whisked egg white and is quite light in texture. Do not be fooled, however: this is a seriously filling dessert with plenty of calories tucked underneath in the butterscotch mixture, made from condensed milk and butter.

FOR 8 PERSONS

1 batch of sweet pastry
  (page 156)
FOR THE FILLING
1 can condensed milk
4 tablespoons cornflour
  (cornstarch)
2 tablespoons plain
  (all-purpose) flour
225g (8oz/1 1/2 cups)
  demerara (brown) sugar
225g (8oz/2 sticks)
  unsalted butter
2 medium (large) eggs
FOR THE TOPPING
4 tablespoons double
  (heavy) cream
1 tablespoon grated
  chocolate
1 teaspoon ground cinnamon

Heat the oven to 200°C (400°F/Gas 6). Line a 26cm (10in) flan case with the sweet pastry and bake blind for about 15 minutes or until it is thoroughly cooked.

To make the butterscotch filling, warm the condensed milk in a saucepan, then add the cornflour and flour. Stir the mixture over a low heat until almost boiling.

In another pan, heat the sugar and butter together. Boil for a few minutes, then add 225ml (8floz/1 cup) of water to make a syrup. Bring to the boil once more.

Combine the hot syrup with the thickened condensed milk. Reboil the mixture a final time. Separate the eggs, set the whites aside and whisk the yolks into the butterscotch. Pour the mixture into the tart case and leave to cool.

To make the topping, whisk the egg whites and, in a separate bowl, whip the cream. Fold one into the other and spread over the cooled tart. Cover with grated chocolate and cinnamon.

POINTS TO WATCH
You want the pastry case to be thoroughly cooked and perhaps even quite crisp for it will have no further cooking after it is baked blind.

Use a non-stick pan for cooking the condensed milk or you will have a nasty cleaning job to perform afterwards.

CHEESECAKE

Delicious on its own with a cup of coffee, this cheesecake also makes a first-rate dessert if topped with soft summer fruit such as raspberries or blueberries. Like quiches, the image of cheesecakes suffers from the abuse exerted on them over many years by large-scale manufacturers. A well-made, authentic version can be a revelation. You will understand their original appeal once you have stripped away the choc-ripple type of additives usually inflicted on them.

FOR 8 PERSONS

FOR THE PECAN CRUST

150g (5oz) digestive
    biscuits (1 cup graham
    cracker crumbs)
25g (1oz/1 tablespoon)
    pecan nut halves
3 teaspoons caster
    (granulated) sugar
75g (3oz/3/4 stick) butter,
    melted, plus extra for
    greasing

FOR THE FILLING

450g (1lb/2 cups) cream
    cheese, cubed and
    softened
120ml (4floz/1/2 cup)
    soured cream
175g (6oz/scant 1 cup)
    caster (granulated) sugar
3 large (extra-large) eggs
the finely grated zest of
    1 large lemon
1 vanilla bean, split in half
    lengthways

FOR THE TOPPING

350ml (12 1/2floz/1 1/2 cups)
    soured cream
1 tablespoon caster
    (granulated) sugar
1 teaspoon vanilla extract

Prepare the crust by grinding the digestives or graham crackers into fine crumbs in a food processor. Finely chop the pecans and add to the crumbs with the sugar. Pour in the melted butter and mix until thoroughly combined.

Heat the oven to 200°C (400°F/Gas 6). Lightly butter a 23cm (9in) spring-form tin. Press the pecan mixture in an even layer along the bottom of the tin and about 2.5cm (1in) up the side. Bake for 10 minutes, then leave to cool.

Set the oven to 180°C (350°F/Gas 4). Prepare the filling by beating the cream cheese and soured cream until smooth. Gradually beat in the sugar, then the eggs one by one. Beat in the lemon zest and the seeds scraped from the vanilla bean.

Pour the filling into the crust and bake for 45 minutes until firm at the centre. Remove from the oven and cool for 15 minutes.

Raise the oven temperature to 220°C (425°F/Gas 7). Make the topping by mixing together the soured cream, sugar and vanilla extract. Spread evenly over the top of the cheesecake and return to the oven for a further 7 minutes. Remove from the oven and cool for at least 2 hours before serving.

POINTS TO WATCH

The filling here is deliberately quite thin. It may look like it will never set but have patience because it will.

PEAR AND PECAN UPSIDE DOWN CAKE

The combination of pear, pecan and caramel is an American classic. William and Comice are the traditional cooking pears and good new varieties are constantly coming onto the market but you should avoid Conference pears as their texture is too hard for this dish.

FOR 8 PERSONS

FOR THE TOPPING

4 pears, such as William or Comice, peeled, cored and cut into 2cm (3/4in) slices

the finely grated zest and juice of 1 lemon

100g (3 1/2oz/7 tablespoons) unsalted butter

125g (4 1/2oz/heaping 3/4 cup) caster (granulated) sugar

1/2 teaspoon ground ginger

1/2 teaspoon vanilla extract

100g (3 1/2oz/1 cup) pecan nut halves

FOR THE CAKE

75g (3oz/3/4 stick) unsalted butter, softened

225g (8oz/1 heaping cup) caster (granulated) sugar

4 medium (large) eggs, separated

1/2 teaspoon vanilla extract

150g (5oz/1 heaping cup) plain (all-purpose) flour

1 1/2 teaspoons baking powder

1 teaspoon bicarbonate of soda (baking soda)

1/2 teaspoon salt

TO SERVE

thick cream or ice cream

To make the topping, toss the sliced pears with the lemon juice and zest. Melt the butter in a heavy saucepan, then add the pears and cook gently for 3 minutes, stirring occasionally. Stir in the sugar, ginger and vanilla, extract and cook for 10 minutes.

Remove the pears from the saucepan and place in a bowl. Bring the remaining juices to the boil and simmer until they form a thick, dark syrup. Mix this with the pears and pecans and spread along the base of a greased 25cm (10in) cake tin.

For the cake, cream the softened butter and sugar together. Beat in the egg yolks one at a time, then add the vanilla extract. In a separate container, mix all the dry ingredients together and slowly add them to the egg mixture so that it forms a stiff batter.

Heat the oven to 190°C (375°F/Gas 5). Whisk the egg whites until stiff and fold them into the cake batter. Spoon the batter over the pears and pecans in the cake tin. Smooth the top over with a spatula and bake for 35 minutes.

Remove the cake from the oven and let it stand for 5 minutes before turning upside down onto a serving platter. Serve the cake warm, with some thick cream or ice cream.

GINGERED NECTARINE AND BLUEBERRY SUMMER PUDDING

Made with brioche rather than plain white bread and spiked with a knob of root ginger, the similarities between this dish and the original summer pudding lie in it being pressed so that the juices from the fruit soak into the bread.

FOR 4 – 6 PERSONS

225g (8oz/1 heaping cup)
*   caster (granulated) sugar*
a small knob of fresh ginger,
*   peeled*
4 ripe nectarines, stoned
*   and cut into 3cm (1 1/4in)*
*   wedges*
4 ripe plums, stoned
*   and cut into 3cm (1 1/4in)*
*   wedges*
3 punnets (about 3 cups)
*   blueberries*
1 tablespoon lemon juice
8 slices brioche, 2cm (3/4in)
*   thick*
TO SERVE
crème fraîche or ice cream

Place the sugar and ginger in a large saucepan with 175ml (6floz/3/4 cup) of water. Bring to the boil, stirring until the sugar has dissolved. Stir in the prepared fruit and simmer for 5 minutes.

Remove the pan from the heat and stir in the lemon juice. Transfer the mixture to a shallow dish for quick cooling and, when the fruit is cool, discard the ginger.

Heat the oven to 200°C (400°F/Gas 6). Lay the brioche slices on a baking tray in one layer and toast them until golden brown on both sides, turning them over halfway through if necessary. Afterwards, transfer to a wire rack to cool.

Arrange one-third of the brioche slices along the bottom of a deep serving dish – 20cm (8in) square is ideal – and then pour on half the cooled fruit mixture. Cover with more brioche, then the rest of the fruit, and finally the remaining brioche.

Cover the pudding with plastic wrap, weigh down the surface evenly and chill overnight. Before serving, remove the weights and plastic wrap, cut the pudding into portions and serve with a little crème fraîche or ice cream.

POINTS TO WATCH
The pudding needs to be weighted evenly over its surface with something around 2kg (4lb 8oz) – perhaps another serving dish of the same size filled with cutlery or similar.

There will almost certainly be some spillage of dark red fruit juice as the pudding is pressed, so place a tray underneath it in the refrigerator.

CHOCOLATE MARJOLAINE

The original version of this dessert was a speciality of the Pyramide restaurant in Vienne, France. In this recipe I have the altered proportions so that there is much more chocolate to baked meringue – I prefer it that way. It's a fairly complex method and requires your total attention while being made.

FOR 8 PERSONS

FOR THE WHITE LAYER

75g (3oz/3/4 cup) white
   chocolate couverture
2 tablespoons milk
a drop of vanilla extract
10g (1/2oz/1 sachet)
   powdered gelatine
2 medium (large) egg yolks
50g (2oz/1/3 cup) caster
   (granulated) sugar
150ml (5floz/2/3 cup)
   double (heavy) cream
150ml (5floz/2/3 cup)
   soured cream

FOR THE MERINGUE

75g (3oz/heaping 1/2 cup)
   blanched hazelnuts
50g (2oz/scant 1/2 cup)
   blanched almonds
50g (2oz/1/3 cup) caster
   (granulated) sugar
1 tablespoon plain
   (all-purpose) flour
3 medium (large) egg whites

FOR THE DARK LAYER

175g (6oz/1 1/2 cups) dark
   chocolate couverture
2 tablespoons brewed coffee
3 tablespoons caster
   (granulated) sugar
75g (3oz/3/4 stick) unsalted
   butter

To prepare the white layer, grate the white chocolate and gently melt it in a saucepan with the milk and vanilla extract. Meanwhile, dissolve the gelatine in 6 tablespoons of lukewarm water.

Whisk the egg yolks and sugar in a bowl. When the chocolate has completely melted into the milk, add it to the egg mixture. Return to the saucepan and cook over a gentle heat, whisking continuously, until the mixture thickens – do not let it boil.

Add one-third of the gelatine mixture and leave to cool.

Whisk the cream and soured cream together until firm, and add half of this to the white chocolate mixture. Place in the refrigerator so that it may begin to set.

Heat the oven to 180°C (350°F/Gas 4). To make the almond and hazelnut meringue, grind together the nuts, then combine them with the sugar and flour.

Whisk the egg whites until firm and fold them into the nut mixture. Spread the mixture on a baking tray lined with non-stick baking parchment and bake for 12 minutes.

To make the dark layer, grate the dark chocolate and gently melt it in a saucepan with the coffee and sugar. Stir in the butter and turn off the heat. Add the remaining gelatine mixture and leave to cool. Fold in the remaining whisked creams.

To assemble the marjolaine, line a terrine or oblong cake tin with plastic wrap. Pour in half the dark chocolate mixture. Cut the cooked meringue into 2 rectangles and place one on top of the chocolate. Cover with all the white chocolate mixture and lay the second rectangle of meringue on top of this. Spread over the remaining dark chocolate mixture and refrigerate overnight to set. Serve the marjolaine in slices.

POINTS TO WATCH

The dark chocolate mixture sets more quickly than the white so make the white layer first.

Chocolate is sensitive to heat and will become streaky if warmed too fast. Go slowly.

Couverture is the word for professional cooking chocolate. Dark couverture comes in various grades from 50 percent cocoa solids to 70 percent (which has very little sugar), and 100 percent (which has none). Generally, the higher the percentage, the better the product. Couverture is more expensive than standard chocolate bars.

SOMLOI

Somloi is Hungary's answer to sherry trifle. It's very rich, so a small portion is all that's needed, but as it's not worth making just four portions at a time, this recipe will deliver somloi for eight. You can always invite more friends round if this is a problem, or eat it two days in succession.

FOR 8 PERSONS

FOR THE SPONGE

4 small (medium) eggs

100g (3 1/2oz/1/2cup) caster
   (granulated) sugar

100g (3 1/2oz/3/4 cup) plain
   (all-purpose) flour

FOR THE PASTRY CREAM

175g (6oz/heaping 3/4 cup)
   caster (granulated) sugar

8 medium (large) egg yolks

750ml (1 pint 6floz/3 1/4 cups)
   milk

1 vanilla bean, split

50g (2oz/scant 1/3 cup) plain
   (all-purpose) flour

FOR THE PASTE

75g (3oz/3/4 cup) walnuts

100g (3 1/2oz/heaping
   1/4 cup) apricot jam

6 tablespoons rum

TO DECORATE

50g (2oz/1/3 cup) dark
   chocolate, in pieces

1 tablespoon butter

300ml (11floz/1 1/3 cups)
   double (heavy) cream

First make the sponge. Heat the oven to 190°C (375°F/Gas 5). Whisk the eggs and sugar together to ribbon stage – when the mixture is thick enough to form a ribbon as the whisk is lifted. Fold in the flour. Transfer the mixture to a square cake tin 5cm (2in) deep and bake for 20 minutes. Remove the cake from the tin and leave to cool on a rack.

To make the pastry cream, whisk half the sugar with the egg yolks. Meanwhile, heat the remaining sugar, milk and vanilla to boiling point. Whisk the flour into the egg mixture, then whisk in the infused hot milk. Remove the vanilla bean and scrape the small black seeds back into the custard. Stir until it returns to the boil, then pour the pastry cream into a bowl to cool.

Grind the walnuts to breadcrumb-size, then add the apricot jam and rum and mix well.

Slice the sponge cake horizontally into two 2cm (3/4in) layers. Spread both with the walnut paste, then place a layer of the sponge, sticky side up, into a deep dish. Pour on the pastry cream and top with another layer of sponge, sticky side down this time. Refrigerate until cool or, better, overnight.

To decorate, gently melt the chocolate and butter together. Lightly whip the cream. Cut the somloi into squares and place on serving dishes. Cover with a large spoonful of whipped cream, then drizzle with the melted chocolate.

POINTS TO WATCH

If the jam is particularly solid, you may need to warm it before mixing it into the ground walnuts. With a soft-set jam, this should not be necessary.

LEMON POSSET

In the late sixties and early seventies, this was a regular dessert at Robert Carrier's esteemed restaurant in Islington. It looks rather like syllabub but is lighter and tastes much fresher.

FOR 6 – 8 PERSONS

2 lemons
150ml (5floz/2/3 cup) dry
  white wine
5 tablespoons caster
  (granulated) sugar
2 egg whites
600ml (1 pint/22/3 cups)
  double (heavy) cream
6-8 brandysnaps or tuiles
  (pages 184 and 187)

Grate the zest of both lemons into a bowl. Squeeze the juice and sieve it into the bowl. Stir in the wine and sugar.

Whisk the egg whites until stiff and dry. Set aside.

In a separate bowl, whip the cream. As it thickens, trickle in the lemon mixture. Continue whisking until stiff.

Fold the whisked egg whites into the cream, then pipe or spoon the posset into serving glasses. Serve accompanied by the crisp tuiles or brandysnap biscuits.

POINTS TO WATCH
Lemon posset will keep for up to a day in the fridge. If it begins to separate, it can be rescued by re-whisking but there will be a small loss in volume.

ICED PEAR WILLIAM PARFAIT

Iced parfaits are ideal for those who have no ice cream maker to churn custard into ice cream or syrup into sorbet. The word parfait signifies little, but in the absence of any other term has come to denote smooth-textured confections such as this, whether eaten hot or cold.

FOR 6 – 8 PERSONS

750g (1lb 10oz) pears,
  preferably William
1 tablespoon lemon juice
250g (9oz/1 1/4 cups) caster
  (granulated) sugar
4 medium (large) egg whites
300ml (11floz/1 1/3 cups)
  double (heavy) cream
1 1/2 tablespoons poire
  William eau de vie
6-8 brandysnaps or tuiles
  (pages 184 and 187)

Peel and core the pears, then cut them into small pieces. Mix with the lemon juice in a small saucepan. Cover and stew the pears over a low heat until soft. Transfer the cooked fruit to a food processor and blend until smooth.

Heat the sugar with 125ml (4floz/1/2 cup) of water in a saucepan over a low heat. When the sugar has dissolved, increase the heat and boil hard for 3 to 4 minutes.

Whisk the egg whites until stiff, then beat in the hot syrup. In a separate bowl, whip the cream and fold it into the egg white mixture. Then fold in the pear purée and eau de vie.

Line an oblong loaf tin or terrine mould with plastic wrap. Spoon in the parfait mixture and freeze overnight. Serve in slices about 2cm (3/4in) thick, with a tuile or brandysnap.

POINTS TO WATCH
Before slicing the finished parfait, dip your knife in hot water to help cut smoothly.

A third of the money spent in a restaurant will be on wine, bottled water and booze, but mostly wine. Restaurateurs love this for there is little effort in uncorking a bottle and, for the person who chooses wine for the list, a pleasurable tasting process that can be passed off as work. Work can also be invented to justify price mark-ups on wine. The razzmatazz of decanting at table and pouring the wine a sip at a time from an ice bucket half a mile away adds a sense of occasion to a meal for those who like that sort of thing.

The truth though is that you are not buying a bottle of wine in a restaurant in the same way as you might in an off-licence or supermarket. Instead you are buying a meal, usually with wine, and the profit on the final bill has to cover the cost of things other than the food and wine consumed – the attention of a waiter for the evening for instance. Try asking for a table in the drinks aisle at Tesco and a member of staff to pour your vino: the response could be cool. Given all this, wine is still too expensive in most restaurants and this is a pity for it means that people have to drink lesser wines than a good meal might deserve.

Mostly it is men who choose the wine in restaurants. It's one of those things, like carving the Sunday joint or cremating sausages on a barbecue, that is perceived as male territory, by men anyway, and there is loss of face if advice has to be asked. The result is that most people make safe but uninspired choices, such as middle range white Loire wines and Rhône reds. Diners need not feel uncomfortable in these situations. Only the crassest wine waiters think that the choice of a hugely expensive wine indicates the presence of a great gourmet and a wine list that doesn't have good drinking at the cheap end reflects badly on the restaurant.

There is a logic to the procedures that follow ordering your wine in a restaurant and it is always appreciated by the staff if the traditions are understood. The bottle is presented so that you can check the label to see that the wine presented is what you ordered and the correct vintage, not so that the bottle may be felt and some comment on its temperature made. The sip of wine given to whoever chooses the bottle is for checking on the wine's condition – a sniff will tell you if it is corked or oxidized – and not to see whether you like it or not.

Lastly, rest assured that no wine will perfectly match the food of a table of four who are all eating something different, so don't worry about it. And enjoy – it's meant to be a treat.

LEMON CRÈME CARAMELS WITH POACHED PEAR

Here is an agreeable take on an old favourite, with citrus flavours providing the focal point. Grilled or poached peaches may be substituted for the pears in summer.

FOR 4 PERSONS

FOR THE CARAMEL
100g (3 1/2 oz/1/2 cup)
  granulated sugar
FOR THE CUSTARD
400ml (14floz/1 3/4 cups)
  milk
the finely grated zest of
  1 lemon
a few drops of vanilla extract
6 medium (large) egg yolks
75g (3oz/scant 1/2 cup)
  caster (granulated) sugar
FOR THE PEARS
4 pears, preferably William
  or Comice, peeled, cored
  and sliced
a little caster (confectioners')
  sugar, for sprinkling

First make the caramel. Place the sugar in a saucepan with 2 tablespoons of water and dissolve over a low heat. Bring to the boil and boil hard until you have a light caramel. Lift the pan from the heat and let the colour deepen to a dark caramel. Pour into four ramekins or dariole moulds.

Heat the oven to 180°C (350°F/Gas 4). To make the custard, heat the milk in a saucepan with the lemon zest and vanilla extract. In a mixing bowl, whisk the egg yolks and sugar together, then whisk in the hot milk.

Pour the custard into the ramekins and place in a roasting tray half-filled with hot water. Cover with parchment paper and bake for 35 minutes. Remove from the tray and leave to cool.

Sprinkle the sliced pears with sugar then grill until the sugar melts and starts to brown the pears. Turn out the crème caramels, lay the slices of grilled pear alongside and serve.

POINTS TO WATCH
The colour of the caramel has a big effect on the balance of the dish. A dark caramel has a richer, more bitter flavour than a pale caramel, which will taste sickly sweet. The ideal here is a deep brown colour with no trace of black.

CRÈME BRÛLÉE WITH RASPBERRIES

In recent years it has been impossible to avoid crème brûlée. It adorns menus throughout the world and comes with every imaginable flavouring, some nice and some nasty. Don't let this put you off, the fact is it makes a fine dessert, but raspberries are the only addition to the basic recipe that I enjoy.

FOR 6 PERSONS

400ml (14floz/1 3/4 cups)
double (heavy) cream
100ml (3 1/2 floz/1/2 cup)
milk
1 vanilla bean, split in half
lengthways
4 medium (large) egg yolks
3 tablespoons caster
(granulated) sugar
1 punnet (1 cup) raspberries
caster (granulated) sugar,
for dusting

Heat the cream, milk and vanilla bean to boiling point in a saucepan. In a large jug or bowl, whisk the egg yolks and sugar together, then whisk in the cream mixture.

Heat the oven to 180°C (350°F/Gas 3). Divide the raspberries between six ramekins, then pour in the cream mixture. Place the ramekins in a roasting tray half-filled with hot water and bake for 45 minutes or until the custards have set.

Lift the ramekins onto a wire rack to cool. Just before serving, spread a thin layer of sugar across the top of each ramekin and caramelize with a kitchen blowtorch.

POINTS TO WATCH

If you have no blowtorch, the crème brûlées may be arranged in a deep dish, surrounded by cold water and ice cubes, then placed under a hot grill or broiler. The ice prevents the custard underneath from hardening.

RHUBARB AND STRAWBERRY GRATIN

Rhubarb and strawberries marry well, especially if you can use the last of the forced rhubarb with the first home-grown strawberries. This dish has contrasts of texture and temperature, cold sorbet inside and crisp, gratinated, sugar on the surface – a bit like a baked Alaska.

FOR 4 PERSONS

FOR THE SORBET

160g (5 1/2 oz/2/3 cup) caster (granulated) sugar

250g (9oz/1 3/4 cups) forced rhubarb, cut into 2cm (3/4in) pieces

the juice of 1 lemon

FOR THE CUSTARD

90g (3 1/2 oz/1/2 cup) caster (granulated) sugar

375ml (13floz/1 2/3 cups) milk

a few drops of vanilla extract

4 egg yolks

25g (1oz/scant 1/4 cup) plain (all-purpose) flour

100ml (3 1/2 floz/1/2 cup) double (heavy) cream

FOR THE COMPOTE

250g (9oz/1 3/4 cups) forced rhubarb, cut into 2cm (3/4in) pieces

100g (3 1/2 oz/1/2 cup) caster (granulated) sugar

1 punnet (1 cup) strawberries

TO FINISH

4 tablespoons caster (granulated) sugar, for sprinkling

First make the sorbet. In a saucepan, combine the sugar with 160ml (5 1/2 floz/2/3 cup) of water and bring to the boil to make a sugar syrup. Set aside to cool.

Cook the rhubarb with 2 tablespoons of water for 5 minutes. Cool, then mix with the sugar syrup and purée in a blender. Add the lemon juice and place in the fridge to chill. When very cold, churn the mixture in an ice cream machine, or simply freeze.

To make the custard, heat half the sugar with the milk and vanilla extract. Meanwhile whisk the remaining sugar with the egg yolks. Whisk the flour into the yolk mixture and, when the milk reaches boiling point, whisk it onto the yolk mixture too. Return the custard to the saucepan and stir just until it comes to the boil. Pour into a bowl to cool.

To make the compote, cook the rhubarb with the sugar and 2 tablespoons of water. Spoon the cooked rhubarb and the strawberries onto 4 serving dishes. Put a scoop of rhubarb sorbet at the centre of each.

Whisk the cream until stiff, then fold it into the custard. Spoon this over the fruit and sorbet. Sprinkle with sugar and caramelize either with a blowtorch or under a hot grill or broiler.

POINTS TO WATCH

If you don't have an ice cream machine, you can 'still-freeze' the sorbet. To do this, freeze the mixture for an hour, then either beat it or blend it in a food processor. Return to the freezer and repeat the process after another hour.

CINNAMON FRENCH TOAST WITH RUM AND RAISIN ICE CREAM

This is either a very simple recipe or a complex one. It depends on how much you buy in. Serviceable brioche and fine ice creams are on sale in most supermarkets, but the intrepid will want to accomplish the entire dish themselves. They know that leftover brioche will freeze for use another day and that the investment in an ice cream machine is wasted if nothing is ever made in the thing.

FOR 4 PERSONS

FOR THE ICE CREAM

4 heaped tablespoons raisins

4 tablespoons rum

4 medium (large) egg yolks

110g (4oz/heaping 1/2 cup)
  caster (granulated) sugar

275ml (10floz/1 1/4 cups) milk

a few drops of vanilla extract

275ml (10floz/1 1/4 cups)
  double (heavy) cream

FOR THE FRENCH TOAST

150ml (5floz/2/3 cup) double
  (heavy) cream

2 whole medium (large)
  eggs, plus 1 egg yolk

1 tablespoon caster
  (granulated) sugar

1/2 teaspoon ground cinnamon

8 slices brioche loaf

1 tablespoon butter

icing (confectioners') sugar,
  for dusting

To begin the ice cream, soak the raisins in the rum. In a separate bowl, whisk the egg yolks and sugar together until white.

In a saucepan, heat the milk and vanilla extract together until nearly boiling then whisk onto the egg yolks and sugar. Return the pan to a gentle heat and stir constantly until the custard thickens perceptibly – this happens just below boiling point.

Strain the custard into a bowl, stir in the cream and leave to cool. When cold, add the soaked raisins and churn until frozen.

To make the french toast, whisk the cream, eggs, sugar and cinnamon together in a large bowl, then dip the brioche slices in this creamy batter.

Melt some butter in a frying pan. When it starts to colour, fry the brioche on each side until brown. Lift onto paper towels and dust with icing sugar. Serve with the ice cream.

POINTS TO WATCH

Most ice creams can be made without churning. The result will not be as smooth but will be a pleasure to eat nonetheless. You need to pre-freeze the bowl into which the cooled custard is poured and then put it in the freezer. Afterwards, give the mixture a good stir every half hour until it is frozen.

The recipe for honey bread on page 22 can be used for the brioche if 3 level tablespoons of sugar is substituted for the honey used in that loaf.

WINTER FRUIT COMPOTE WITH RICE PUDDING ICE CREAM

Fruit compote has a deeply unsexy image as a boarding house breakfast. Even so, winter fruit such as apples and pears lightly stewed with dried summer specimens such as apricots can make a surprisingly effective and appropriate dessert on a December day, when the idea of imported strawberries and raspberries from the southern hemisphere seems daft.

The ice cream recipe will yield almost a litre, a generous amount for just four portions of compote, but it is not worth making any smaller quantity. Of course any leftovers will be good another time.

FOR 4 PERSONS

FOR THE RICE PUDDING
375ml (13floz/1 3/4 cups)
    milk
100g (3 1/2 oz/1/2 cup)
    caster (granulated) sugar
50g (2oz/scant 1/4 cup)
    pudding rice
a pinch of salt

FOR THE ICE CREAM
500ml (18floz/2 1/4 cups)
    milk
2 vanilla beans, split in half
    lengthways
6 egg yolks
150g (5oz/3/4 cup) caster
    (granulated) sugar
250ml (9floz/1 cup) double
    (heavy) cream

FOR THE COMPOTE
2 apples, preferably Cox's
    orange pippin
2 pears, preferably William
8 ready-to-eat dried apricots
100ml (3 1/2 floz/1/2 cup)
    apple juice
3 level tablespoons caster
    (granulated) sugar
1 cinnamon stick

TO SERVE
4 brandysnaps (page 184)

To make the rice pudding, put all the ingredients in a saucepan, bring to the boil and simmer until the rice is cooked, about 25 minutes, stirring regularly to prevent sticking. Transfer the rice pudding to a bowl to cool.

For the ice cream, heat the milk and split vanilla beans in a saucepan. When the milk comes to the boil, remove from the heat. Fish out the vanilla beans and scrape the small black seeds back into the milk.

Whisk the egg yolks and sugar together in a large bowl until the mixture pales in colour. Then slowly, carefully, and while still whisking, trickle the hot milk onto the egg mixture.

Return this custard to a low heat and cook, stirring continuously, until it slightly but perceptibly thickens. Stir in the cream and set aside until cool.

When cold, combine the custard with the cooked rice pudding and churn the resulting mixture in an ice cream maker.

To make the fruit compote, peel and core the apple and pears. Cut them into quarters and place in a saucepan with the dried apricots, apple juice, sugar and cinnamon. Bring to the boil, then cover the pan and simmer gently for about 5 minutes or until the fruit is cooked but still firm. Leave to cool.

Serve the fruit compote with the ice cream and brandysnaps.

Canapés, amuse-gueules and petits fours

Canapés may seem fancy but in fact they are practical. There is a time gap between when people arrive and when any food will be ready. At The Merchant House we have no bar for people to sit at, so customers go straight to the table and, rather than have them simply stare at each other, or eat two baskets of bread so that they're not hungry anymore, we present a small plateful of snacks to assuage the intervening pangs without too much damage to over-all appetite. Home cooks essentially do the same thing in offering olives and nuts.

Canapés aren't really a part of the meal at all and should be small enough not to inter-fere with its balance or structure. They usually partner a drink, so in order to compete with a flute of champagne or the power of a martini cocktail, they must be robustly flavoured. No cutlery or napkins should be necessary either. The word canapé meant sofa in French and conjures up an unappealing image of cold toast cut in small pieces, covered with mean amounts of smoked salmon, then coated in aspic. Unfortunately there is, as yet, no better word to describe the bite-sized morsels that fend off stomach rumblings whilst you swallow an aperitif or two. Certainly cold toast need not feature and there is the opportunity to use any small scraps of pastry you have in the fridge to hold whatever filling you choose.

Cold toast need not feature.

An amuse-gueule (or amuse-bouche) is a restaurant device that also allows the kitchen time to put together your first course. It is a ready-made, no-choice snacklet that can be pre-sented as a gift from the chef and gives the kitchen an extra ten minutes during which they know that you have actually sat down and started eating. Usually amuse-gueules are minia-ture starters and almost anything that can be shrunk down to two mouthfuls will fill the bill.

There is no serviceable English word to cover petit four, although I have seen them described rather coyly as sweetmeats on menus that like to keep things as British as possi-ble. The problem with anything served at the tail end of a meal is that no one is hungry. Small is therefore beautiful if you are not to waste both work and ingredients, the contradiction being that petits fours can take a lot of effort. We've been known to serve sweets found on holidays abroad along with our home-made items such as candied peel (page 186) and chocolate truffles (page 189). Like canapés, petits fours should be intensely flavoured as they are usually consumed with coffee and digestifs.

We do all this, partly because people expect it, yes, and partly because they are part of the traditional progression of the meal. But restaurants – and dinner parties – are about more than serving the correct amount of grub. They are also about generosity.

PIZZA SQUARES

Pizza is made from bread dough rolled into discs and our basic white bread dough makes an excellent version. This recipe calls for the pizza to be baked with only garlic and olive oil on top as a fresh salad is to be spread on afterwards. A square of good puff pastry, rolled out thinly and pricked to avoid rising, will substitute if that is more convenient for you.

FOR 4 PERSONS

FOR THE BASES

1/2 batch of basic white
*   bread dough (page 16)*
1 clove garlic, halved
1 tablespoon olive oil

FOR THE TOPPING

20 anchovy-stuffed green
*   olives*
10 pitted black olives
4 tomatoes, skinned,
*   deseeded and diced*
2 tablespoons grated
*   Parmigiano Reggiano*
*   cheese*
2 tablespoons roughly
*   chopped flat-leaf parsley*
1 tablespoon capers
1 tablespoon olive oil
1 clove garlic, crushed
freshly ground pepper

Heat the oven to 200°C (400°F/Gas 6). Roll out the dough to form a flat disc. Rub the surface with garlic and brush it with the olive oil. Bake for 10 minutes.

Cut the stuffed and black olives into fine dice and mix them with the tomatoes, cheese, parsley, capers, olive oil and garlic. Season the mixture with plenty of milled black pepper.

Cut the baked pizza dough into squares and spoon the tomato and olive salad on top. Serve.

POINTS TO WATCH
Do not chop the olive and tomato salad too finely. A little texture improves the dish.

DEEP-FRIED WONTONS WITH RICOTTA

These taste like deep-fried pasta, which is what the Italians would traditionally use for this type of dish. However, my friend Franco Taruschio, of The Walnut Tree Inn, uses wonton wrappers, which strikes me as eminently sensible as the size of the wrappers is ideal for canapés. You can buy them at any Oriental grocers and even in some large supermarkets.

FOR 4 PERSONS

125g (4oz/1/2 cup) ricotta
*   cheese*
1 teaspoon lemon juice
1 tablespoon chopped basil
*   leaves*
12 wonton wrappers
sunflower oil, for deep-frying

Mix the ricotta, lemon juice and basil together in a bowl. Place a teaspoon of the mixture at the centre of each wonton, then twist the ends in opposite directions to form the shape of an old toffee wrapper.

Heat the oil in a wok or other large pan and when hot, deep-fry the wontons in batches until golden brown.

POINTS TO WATCH

The oil needs to be hot but not smoking. Cooking the wontons in batches ensures that the temperature of the oil remains constant.

MARINATED FRESH SALMON WITH CELERIAC

Salmon is a classic choice for canapés and is a fish that takes to being eaten raw without a lot of marinating. It works well with the clean-tasting mixture of celeriac and horseradish, providing a good contrasting texture. You could put this combination on pieces of toast or pastry as well.

FOR 4 PERSONS

1/2 small celeriac (celery root)
1 tablespoon crème fraîche
1 teaspoon creamed
*   horseradish*
the juice of 1 lemon
2 tablespoons olive oil
100g (31/2oz) raw salmon
*   fillet*
salt and pepper

Peel and dice the celeriac. Boil it in a saucepan of water until tender, then drain.

Blend the celeriac in a food processor with the crème fraîche, horseradish and some seasoning. Add half the lemon juice and 1 tablespoon of olive oil and mix again.

Thinly slice the salmon. Brush the slices with 1 tablespoon of olive oil and the remaining lemon juice.

Put a teaspoon of the celeriac mixture into the middle of each slice of salmon. Roll into the shape of a small cigar and serve.

POINTS TO WATCH

Your salmon must be very fresh in order to be served this way.
    Use tweezers to remove any pin bones from the fish fillet.
    Carefully slice the fish with a sharp carving knife – a serrated knife will hack the flesh.
    The salmon needs to be brushed with marinade only just before serving as the lemon and oil will cook it if left for longer than 15 minutes.

EMPANADILLAS

These are part of the Spanish tapas repertoire. The idea is that tiny amounts of well-flavoured fish and shellfish are mixed with sauce and spooned into puff pastry and deep-fried.

FOR 4 PERSONS

200g (7oz) puff pastry
sunflower oil, for deep-frying
FOR THE FILLING
1 tablespoon chopped
*   shallot*
1 tablespoon finely diced
*   red bell pepper*
25g (1oz/1/4 cup) shelled
*   cooked prawns or shrimp*
25g (1oz/1/4 cup) cod fillet,
*   finely diced*
1 scallop, finely diced
1 teaspoon tomato passata
*   (sieved tomatoes)*
a small pinch of saffron
1/2 teaspoon plain
*   (all-purpose) flour*
1 tablespoon double
*   (heavy) cream*
1 teaspoon Irish whiskey
1 teaspoon chopped
*   coriander (cilantro) leaves*
a dash of Tabasco sauce
salt and pepper

Roll out the puff pastry as thinly as possible, then cut 12 circles about 7cm (2³/₄in) in diameter.

To make the filling, fry the shallot and bell pepper in a small saucepan. Add the seafood, passata and saffron.

Stir in the flour, then add the cream, whiskey and coriander. Season with salt, pepper and some Tabasco sauce and leave the mixture to cool.

Put a teaspoon of filling at the centre of each puff pastry circle. Moisten the edges of the pastry with water and fold across to form a miniature Cornish pasty.

In a wok or similar large pan, heat the oil until it is hot but not smoking. Deep-fry the empanadillas in batches for about 2 minutes or until they are golden brown.

POINTS TO WATCH

This is not the moment to use the fine puff pastry you have made by hand. The commercial product manufactured with industrial-grade margarine actually fries better than pastry made with unsalted butter and top quality flour.

SESAME AND ROQUEFORT BISCUITS

SESAME AND ROQUEFORT BISCUITS

I have been making these easy savoury cheese biscuits for years. They need to be the size of one bite rather than two as they create lots of crumbs and are best served straight from the oven.

MAKES 20

100g (3 1/2oz/7 tablespoons) unsalted butter
100g (3 1/2 oz) self-raising flour (3/4 cup all-purpose flour + 3/4 teaspoon baking powder)
100g (3 1/2 oz/3/4 cup) Roquefort or Stilton cheese
50g (2oz/1/2 cup) sesame seeds

Using a food processor, blend the butter and flour together until the mixture resembles breadcrumbs.

Crumble the cheese and add it to the bowl. Process for another 2-3 seconds only, then knead the mixture once or twice to evenly distribute the ingredients. (The mixture can now be refrigerated until needed.)

Heat the oven to 180°C (350°F/Gas 4). Pinch out small pieces of the dough then roll them into balls about 2.5cm (1in) across. Toss them in the sesame seeds, then space them out on a baking sheet and bake for about 10 minutes or until firm.

POINTS TO WATCH
The mixture will keep for days in the fridge and can be rolled into balls and baked as and when needed.

MARINATED CHICKEN ON STICKS

Small cubes of chicken marinate quickly and provide a vehicle for robust spicing, especially if they are to be eaten in small quantity as here. These can be served hot or cold.

FOR 4 PERSONS

1 boneless breast or leg of chicken
FOR THE MARINADE
2 tablespoons Greek yogurt
1 teaspoon ground cardamon
1 teaspoon lime juice
1/2 small chilli, deseeded and chopped
1 tablespoon flat-leaf parsley, chopped
salt

Combine all the ingredients for the marinade in a bowl. Cut the chicken into 2cm (3/4in cubes) and toss them in the marinade. Leave to stand for 1 hour.

Grill or fry the chicken for 5-10 minutes, until it is browned and crisp outside but still moist and tender inside.

Skewer each piece of chicken with a toothpick and serve.

POINTS TO WATCH
The length of time the chicken cubes will take to cook depends in part on whether you are using breast or the darker, tougher leg meat.

The ground floor of the Merchant House has served as a restaurant for nearly six years now. The majority of that time for me has been spent worrying over trivia, peeling and boiling things, and hoping that the amounts of food we have bought and prepared will coincide with the orders taken in the dining room. It has only rarely involved pondering the meaning of life, gastronomically speaking, or creating a raft of brilliant new dishes with which to dazzle the diners. But it has not been boring.

Each change in the availability of seasonal produce, lobster from Cornwall or game from Shropshire, means rethinking the balance of the menu and the make-up of each dish, scouring recipe books so that others' ideas can be considered and solutions found that suit our own facilities and situation. The goal is for each dish to be stimulating as well as satisfying, at the same time keeping the whole meal more or less in balance.

Once a dish is conceived, it has to be tested and eaten in its entirety to see what works and what doesn't. Needless ingredients and flourishes can then be stripped away so that the main contrasts of flavour and texture are not cluttered, or made subservient to a colour scheme. Restraint and simplicity of execution are central.

If you are thinking of setting up a similar restaurant, you'll be pleased to know that my accountant says we make a profit. Of course, he also says we would make a better one if I were to spend a little less on the victuals and a little more on tax-friendly pension schemes. But then, what does he know about the buzz of a successful evening and the chance of making the next meal a bit better?

MADELEINES

Madeleines were a favourite of Proust and good versions can be bought ready made. You will need to invest in a madeleine tray with small indentations to make petit four-sized versions.

MAKES 12

*100g (3 1/2oz/7 tablespoons)
unsalted butter, plus extra
for greasing*
3 egg whites
*200g (7oz/1 cup) caster
(granulated) sugar*
*50g (2oz/1/2 cup) plain
(all-purpose) flour*
*50g (2oz/1/2 cup) ground
almonds*
1 tablespoon honey

Heat the butter in a small saucepan until it melts and begins to colour, then set aside to cool.

Whisk the egg whites until stiff. In a separate bowl, mix together the sugar, flour and ground almonds. Fold the dry ingredients into the egg whites and then add the butter and honey.

Melt the extra butter for greasing and brush each indentation of the madeleine pan with it. Fill the indentations with the cake mixture and refrigerate for at least 1 hour.

Heat the oven to 190°C (375°F/Gas 5). Bake the madeleines for 15 minutes. Remove from the oven and leave to stand for 1 to 2 minutes before transferring to a wire rack to cool.

POINTS TO WATCH
The mixture sticks like mad, so brush the madeleine tray liberally with melted butter before filling.

BRANDYSNAPS

Brandysnaps are versatile. Large ones moulded over an upturned sugar bowl will act as container for syllabub and turn a simple ice cream or sorbet into a creditable dessert.

MAKES 20 – 30

*100g (3 1/2oz/1/2 cup)
granulated sugar*
*100g (3 1/2 oz/7 tablespoons)
unsalted butter*
*100g (3 1/2oz/1/4 cup) golden
(corn) syrup*
*100g (3 1/2oz/3/4 cup) plain
(all-purpose) flour*
1 tablespoon lemon juice
1 teaspoon ground ginger
sunflower oil, for greasing

Heat the oven to 190°C (375°F/Gas 5). Melt the sugar, butter and syrup together in a large saucepan. Meanwhile, warm the flour in the oven for a few minutes.

Add the warm flour to the butter mixture along with the lemon juice and ginger and mix together.

Put a spoonful of the mixture onto an oiled baking sheet. Place another 15cm (6in) distant, and continue until you have as many brandysnaps as needed or have used all the mixture.

Bake for around 10 minutes until brown then remove from the oven. As they cool, use a palette knife to lift the brandysnaps off the baking sheet and lay them over a rolling pin to set.

POINTS TO WATCH
The warm flour helps the mixture to blend easily.
   If the brandysnaps set before you have had the opportunity to lay them over the rolling pin, just return them to the oven for a short while to soften.

RASPBERRY AND LEMON CURD TARTLETS

This lemon curd is made with cream rather than butter and has a better texture because of it. The tartlets are baked blind and you can either buy little individual moulds or use a baking pan with indentations, such as a miniature Yorkshire pudding or muffin tin.

MAKES 20

1/2 batch of sweet pastry
  (page 156)
20 raspberries
FOR THE LEMON CURD
5 eggs
200g (/oz/1 cup) caster
  (granulated) sugar
175ml (6floz/3/4 cup)
  double (heavy) cream
the finely grated zest and
  juice of 3 lemons

Heat the oven to 180°C (350°F/Gas 4). Roll out the pastry and use it to line the tartlet tins. Bake blind for 15 minutes, then remove from the oven and leave to cool in the tins.

Make the lemon curd by whisking all the ingredients together in a pan or bowl suspended over boiling water.

Cook, whisking occasionally, until the mixture sets, which will take about 30 minutes. When it is as thick as home-made mayonnaise, turn it out into another container to cool.

Spoon the lemon curd into the tartlets and top each one with a fresh raspberry before serving.

POINTS TO WATCH

The lemon curd is sturdier than you might imagine and does not need constant attention. It won't separate while cooking, providing it is whisked every now and again.

CANDIED PEEL

Candied peel keeps well so makes a handy petit four and is invariably welcomed on the plate as a contrast to chocolate or biscuits (cookies). Grapefruit and tangerine peel can be used instead of orange and the results could be dipped in melted chocolate if you fancy.

MAKES 12 PORTIONS
3 large oranges
550g (1lb 3 1/2oz/2 3/4 cups)
*   caster (confectioners')*
*   sugar*

Slice the bases and tops from the oranges, then cut each one diagonally into quarters. Peel the flesh from each quarter and set aside. Cut the rind into sticks measuring the length of the whole orange and 0.5cm (1/4in) wide.

Cover the rind with cold water and bring slowly to the boil. Simmer for 5 minutes, then drain. Cover with cold water again and repeat the operation another 4 times.

Return the drained orange sticks to the saucepan and add 300g (10 1/2oz/1 1/2 cups) of the sugar. Cook over a low heat for 1 hour, stirring continuously at first, then just frequently, with a wooden spoon.

Set a wire rack on top of a baking tray and spread the orange sticks over the rack to drain off any excess syrup.

When the candied peel is dry, roll it in the remaining sugar and store in an airtight container until needed.

POINTS TO WATCH
Although you do not want all the pith on the finished product, some should be left attached to the rind.

CINNAMON AND PISTACHIO TUILES

Tuiles are another useful item that can serve as an accompaniment to a creamy dessert as well as a petit four. The name derives from the shape, which is reminiscent of the saddle-shaped terracotta roof tiles used in southern France.

MAKES 20

4 egg whites

225g (8oz/1 heaping cup) caster (granulated) sugar

100g (3 1/2oz/7 tablespoons) unsalted butter, melted

1 teaspoon ground cinnamon

100g (3 1/2oz/3/4 cup) plain (all-purpose) flour

50g (2oz/1/2 cup) pistachio nuts, skinned and chopped

sunflower oil, for greasing

Heat the oven to 190°C (375°F/Gas 5). Lightly whisk the egg whites to loosen the texture. Whisk in the sugar, followed by the melted butter, cinnamon and flour.

Oil a baking sheet and put a teaspoon of the mixture onto it. Use the back of a fork to spread the mixture into a circle, then sprinkle on some chopped pistachios. Repeat until you have filled the baking sheet, spacing the tuiles 5cm (2in) apart.

Bake for around 6 minutes or until brown. Lift off the tuiles (which will still be soft) with a palette knife and drape them across a rolling pin so that they set in the traditional shape.

POINTS TO WATCH

As with the brandysnaps, if the tuiles set hard before you have the chance to shape them, place them in the oven for a few minutes to resoften.

Cinnamon and pistachio is a good combination, but almost any sweet spice or nut can be used in this recipe to give the tuiles texture and flavour.

CHOCOLATE TRUFFLES

The mixture for chocolate truffles is called ganache. It's also used in small quantities as a filling for cake and biscuits (cookies) and can be flavoured with almost any liqueur instead of the rum used here. This recipe produces chocolate truffles that aren't sickly sweet. If you prefer something sweeter you will need to melt some caster (confectioners') sugar along with the couverture.

MAKES LOTS

FOR THE GANACHE

*600g (1lb 5oz) dark
chocolate couverture*

*200ml (7floz/3/4 cup)
double (heavy) cream*

*300g (10 1/2oz/1 1/4 cups)
unsalted butter, softened*

50ml (2floz/1/4 cup) rum

FOR THE COATING

*250g (9oz) dark chocolate
couverture*

*300g (10 1/2oz/2 1/2 cups)
cocoa powder*

To make the ganache, grate the chocolate and melt it slowly in a heatproof bowl set over a saucepan of warm water.

Meanwhile, boil the cream in a small saucepan and set it aside to cool. Once cooled, pour the cream into the melted chocolate, beating continuously.

In a large bowl, whisk the softened butter until light, then trickle in the chocolate cream. Continue whisking until well combined, then keep this mixture in the fridge until ready to use.

To prepare the coating, grate and melt the remaining chocolate couverture. Place the cocoa powder in a box or similar container.

Use a small scoop, melon baller or parisienne cutter to make balls of the chilled chocolate ganache. Spear each ball with a toothpick, dip it in the melted chocolate couverture, then roll in the cocoa powder. Store chilled.

POINTS TO WATCH

Do not hurry the melting of the couverture. Chocolate is delicate and will become streaky if it is heated too much.

INDEX

I am indebted to my editor Jenni Muir for the idea of writing this book;
to Vanessa Courtier who made it look just the way I wanted; and to
Jason Lowe, not just for his estimable photographic talent but for the
reassuring way he ate everything photographed and seemed to really enjoy it.
Most of all, I am indebted to Anja, who does half the work here and without
whom The Merchant House restaurant would not be possible.